1 All-Star

Linda Lee

Grace Tanaka ★ Shirley Velasco

Second Edition

Connect
Learn
Succeed™

ALL-STAR 1 STUDENT BOOK

ISBN 978-0-07-338469-6

MHID 0-07-338469-0

ISE ISBN 978-0-07-131382-7

ISE MHID 0-07-131382-6

Vice president/Editor in chief: *Elizabeth Haefele*
Vice president/Director of marketing: *John E. Biernat*
Director of sales and marketing, ESL: *Pierre Montagano*
Director of development: *Valerie Kelemen*
Developmental editors: *Maya Lazarus, Laura LeDrean, Nancy Jordan*
Marketing manager: *Kelly Curran*
Lead digital product manager: *Damian Moshak*
Digital developmental editor: *Kevin White*
Director, Editing/Design/Production: *Jess Ann Kosic*
Lead project manager: *Susan Trentacosti*
Senior production supervisor: *Debra R. Sylvester*
Designer: *Srdjan Savanovic*
Senior photo research coordinator: *Lori Kramer*
Photo researcher: *Allison Grimes*
Digital production coordinator: *Cathy Tepper*
Illustrators: *Alyta Adams, Gioia Fiommenghi, Jerry Gonzalez, Mike Hortens, Andrew Lange, Chris Pappas, Bot Roda, Daniel Rubenstein, Susan Tait-Porcaro, Chris Winn, David Winter, Jerry Zimmerman, Laserwords*
Typeface: *11.5/12.5 Frutiger LT Std 45 Light*
Compositor: *Laserwords Private Limited*
Printer: *Worldcolor*
Cover credit: *Andrew Lange*
Credits: *The credits section for this book begins on page 216 and is considered an extension of the copyright page.*

www.mhhe.com

ACKNOWLEDGMENTS

The authors and publisher would like to thank the following individuals who reviewed *All-Star Second Edition* at various stages of development and whose comments, reviews, and field-testing were instrumental in helping us shape the second edition of the series:

Carlos Alcazar, Newport-Mesa USD Adult School, Costa Mesa, CA ★ Isabel V. Anderson, The English Center, Miami, FL ★ Carol Antunano, The English Center, Miami, FL ★ Ted Anderson ★ Josefina Aucar, Miami Beach Adult and Community Education Center, Miami, FL ★ Veronica Pavon-Baker, Miami Dade County Public Schools, Miami, FL ★ Barry Bakin, Pacoima Skills Center, Pacoima, CA ★ Michael Blackman, Reseda Community Adult School, Reseda, CA ★ Taylor H. Blakely, Newport-Mesa USD Adult School, Costa Mesa, CA ★ Marge Bock, Sweetwater USD Adult Education, Chula Vista, CA ★ Lusine Bokhikyan ★ Rothwell H Bouillon, Pacoima Skills Center, Pacoima, CA ★ Ian Brailsford, South Piedmont Community College, Monroe, NC ★ Roy Carl Brungardt, Riverside Adult School, Riverside, CA ★ Paul Buczko, Pacoima Skills Center, Pacoima, CA ★ Gemma S Burns, Riverside Adult School, Riverside, CA ★ Kathleen Bywater, Riverside Adult School, Riverside, CA ★ Helen Canellos, Milwaukee Area Technical College, Milwaukee, WI ★ Richard H Capet, Pimmit Hills Adult Education Center, Falls Church, VA ★ Waldo Cardenas, Miami Dade County Public Schools, Miami, FL ★ Gemma Santos Catire, Miami Beach Adult and Community Education Center, Miami, FL ★ Julio Chow, Pacoima Skills Center, Pacoima, CA ★ Claire Cirolia, Fairfax County Adult ESL Program, Fairfax, VA ★ Sabine Cooke, Riverside Adult School, Riverside, CA ★ Jeffrey R Corrigan, Newport-Mesa USD Adult School, Costa Mesa, CA ★ Don Curtis, Oakland USD Adult Education, Neighborhood Centers, Oakland, CA ★ Angela DeRocco, Sweetwater USD Adult Education, Chula Vista, CA ★ Jorge de la Paz, Miami Sunset Adult Center, Miami, FL ★ Deborah Ebersold, Pacoima Skills Center, Pacoima, CA ★ Fernando Egea, Miami Sunset Adult Center, Miami, FL ★ Marilyn Farrell, Riverside Adult School, Riverside, CA ★ Lora Finch, Newport-Mesa USD Adult School, Costa Mesa, CA ★ Pat Fox, Montgomery College, Rockville, MD ★ Antoinette Galaviz, Reseda Community Adult School, Reseda, CA ★ Elizabeth Gellatly, Newport-Mesa USD Adult School, Costa Mesa, CA ★ Dennys Gonzalez, Miami Dade College, Miami, FL ★ Amber G Goodall, South Piedmont Community College, Monroe, NC ★ Amy Grodzienski, Reseda Community Adult School, Reseda, CA ★ Ana Guadayol, Miami-Dade College VESOL, Miami, FL ★ Diane Helvig, Sweetwater USD Adult Education, Chula Vista, CA ★ Kristine Hoffman, Newport-Mesa USD Adult School, Costa Mesa, CA ★ Dr. Coral Horton, Miami-Dade College, Miami, FL ★ Valerie Johnson, Reseda Community Adult School, Reseda, CA ★ Ali Kiani, Reseda Community Adult School, Reseda, CA ★ Donna Kihara, Reseda Community Adult School, Reseda, CA ★ Angela Kosmas, Wilbur Wright College, Chicago, IL ★ Alida Labiosa, Newport-Mesa USD Adult School, Costa Mesa, CA ★ Lourdes A. Laguilles, Reseda Community Adult School, Reseda, CA ★ Holly Lawyer, Elgin Community College, Elgin, Illinois ★ Lia Lerner, Burbank Adult School, Burbank, CA ★ Mae F Liu, Chinese American Planning Council, New York, NY ★ Levia Loftus, College of Lake County, Grayslake, IL ★ Nancy Magathan, Reseda Community Adult School, Reseda, CA ★ Monica Manero-Cohen, Miami Beach Adult and Community Education Center, Miami, FL ★ Matilda Martinez, Miami Beach Adult and Community Education Center, Miami, FL ★ Suzette Mascarenas, Newport-Mesa USD Adult School Costa Mesa, CA ★ Sara McKinnon, College of Marin, Kentfield, CA ★ Ibis Medina, Miami Sunset Adult Center, Miami, FL ★ Alice-Ann Menjivar, Carlos Rosario International Public Charter School, Washington, DC ★ Kathleen Miller, Reseda Community Adult School, Reseda, CA ★ Kent Minault, Pacoima Skills Center, Pacoima, CA ★ Pedro Monteagudo, Miami Beach Adult and Community Education Center, Miami, FL ★ Jose Montes, The English Center, Miami, FL ★ Ilene Mountain, Newport-Mesa USD Adult School Costa Mesa, CA ★ Mary Murphy-Clagett, Sweetwater USD Adult Education, Chula Vista, CA ★ Fransisco Narciso, Reseda Community Adult School, Reseda, CA ★ Anita Nodarse, Miami Dade College, Miami, FL ★ Zoila Ortiz, Miami Sunset Adult Center, Miami, FL ★ Phil Oslin, Sweetwater USD, Adult Education, Chula Vista, CA ★ Nancy Pakdel, Newport-Mesa USD Adult School, Costa Mesa, CA ★ Eduardo Paredes-Ferro, Miami Sunset Adult Center, Miami, FL ★ Virginia Parra, Miami Dade College, Interamerican Campus, Miami, FL ★ Elaine S Paris, Chinese American Planning Council, New York, NY ★ Ellen R. Purcell, Public Schools/Pimmit Hills, Falls Church, VA ★ Michelle R Quiter, Austin Community College, Austin, TX ★ Sandra Ramirez, Pacoima Skills Center, Pacoima, CA ★ Corinne Rennie, Newport-Mesa USD Adult School, Costa Mesa, CA ★ Barbara Rinsler ★ Ray Rivera, South Dade Adult Education Center, Homestead, FL ★ Abdali Safaei, Reseda Community Adult School, Reseda, CA ★ Bernard Sapir, Reseda Community Adult School, Reseda, CA ★ Amy Schneider, Pacoima Skills Center, Pacoima, CA ★ Delisa Sexton, Pacoima Skills Center, Pacoima, CA ★ Norma S Smith, Pacoima Skills Center, Pacoima, CA ★ Mandi M Spottsville, Newport-Mesa USD Adult School ★ Helen G Stein, Miami Dade College, Miami, FL ★ Jennifer C Storm, College of Lake County, Grayslake, IL ★ Terri L Stralow, South Piedmont Community College, Monroe, NC ★ Dina P Tarrab, Reseda Community Adult School, Reseda, CA ★ Maliheh Vafai, East Side Adult Education, San Jose, CA ★ Rosanne Verani, Riverside Adult School, Riverside, CA ★ Kermey Wang, Riverside Adult School, Riverside, CA ★ Cynthia Whisner, Riverside Adult School, Riverside, CA ★ Duane Wong, Newport-Mesa USD Adult School, Costa Mesa, CA

SCOPE AND SEQUENCE

LIFE SKILLS

UNIT	Listening and Speaking	Reading and Writing	Critical Thinking	Vocabulary	Grammar
Pre-Unit Meeting Your Classmates *page 2*	• Listen to introductions • Introduce yourself • Ask for and give spelling of names	• Make a name tag		• Personal information (first, last name) • Alphabet	
Unit 1 Getting Started *page 4*	• Exchange personal information • Talk about things in a classroom • Follow classroom instructions • Say and understand numbers (telephone, area code, zip code) • Use appropriate greetings and partings • Ask about occupations • Introduce people • Pron: Long vowel sounds: *I* and *E* • **WB:** Ask for locations in a school	• Read a world map • Read and write classroom instructions • Read for specific information • Read job ads • Read and complete application forms • Make flashcards • **WB:** Address an envelope	• Classify information • Apply what you know • Interpret information (on an application form) • Interpret a world map	• Classroom vocabulary • Countries • Personal information (name, address, etc.) • Occupations • **WB:** School personnel	• Simple present of *be*, statements • Prepositions of place • Singular and plural nouns • Possessive adjectives
Unit 2 Places *page 18*	• Describe the location of things in the community • Talk about places on a U.S. map • Pron: Intonation patterns • Express lack of comprehension • **WB:** Ask for locations in a school • **WB:** Get someone's attention	• Use a telephone directory • Read a map • Read traffic signs • Write addresses and phone numbers • **WB:** Spotlight: Writing Personal interest stories	• Interpret a map • Classify places (public/private) • Interpret an illustration • Interpret traffic signs	• Geographical directions (N, S, E, W) • Places in the community • Street signs • **WB:** Locations in a school • **WB:** Forms of transportation	• Simple present of *be*, *Wh-* questions • Prepositions of place • *There is/There are* • Capitalization and punctuation
Unit 3 Time and Money *page 32*	• Ask for and tell the time of day • Ask for a phone number from directory assistance • Pron: Syllable stress in numbers • **WB:** Call supervisor to explain tardiness	• Read amounts of money • Read and write personal checks • Read a time schedule • Read signs (in the library) • Write time schedules • Describe a scene • Write amounts of money in words and numbers • **WB:** Complete a time card	• Draw conclusions • Classify information • Compare	• Times of day • Time words • Days of the week • Money: coins and bills • Parts of a personal check • **WB:** Methods of payment	• Simple present of *be*, *Yes/No* questions • Questions with *How much* and *How many* • Capitalization with proper nouns

CORRELATIONS TO STANDARDS

Civics Concepts	Math Skills	CASAS Life Skills Competencies	SCANS Competencies (Workplace)	EFF Content Standards	Florida	LAUSD
		• 0.2.1	• Sociability	• Communicate so that others understand	• 2.01.04	• 1, 9, 58 a
• Identify countries on a map • Recognize different occupations in the community • **WB:** Mail a letter • **WB:** Identify school personnel • **WB:** Identify places in a school	• Use numbers 0 to 11 • Understand page references • Read and write telephone numbers and addresses	• **1:** 0.1.4, 0.2.1, 5.2.5 • **2:** 0.1.2 • **3:** 0.1.2, 0.1.5 • **4:** 0.1.2, 0.2.1, 0.2.2 • **5:** 0.1.4 • **6:** 4.1.3, 4.1.6, 4.1.8 • **WB:** 2.2.2, 2.2.3, 2.4.1	• Know how to learn • See things in the mind's eye • Sociability • Work well with others • Work with people of diverse backgrounds	• Communicate so that others understand • Listen to and learn from others' experiences and ideas	• **3:** 2.01.04 • **4:** 2.01.05 • **5:** 2.01.01, 2.01.02 • **6:** 2.03.01 • **WB:** 2.02.10	• **1:** 1, 5, G1a, G11a • **2:** 15, G14a, G11a • **3:** 15, 18, G5, G9b • **4:** 1, 2, 3, 4, 7, G10c • **5:** 9(a, b, c) • **6:** 50, 51, 52, G9c • **7:** 59 • **WB:** 8, 16, 17
• Identify public services • Locate cities and states in the U.S. • Make a neighborhood map • Identify places in the community • Understand traffic signs • Complete a library card application • Identify forms of transportation	• Understand phone numbers • Read math symbols • Understand spatial relationships	• **1:** 0.1.2, 2.1.1, 2.5.1 • **2:** 0.1.4, 1.2.6, 2.2.1, 2.2.5 • **3:** 1.9.1, 2.2.1, 2.2.2 • **4:** 2.2.1, 2.2.5, 5.2.4 • **5:** 0.1.2, 0.1.4, 0.1.6 • **6:** 2.5.6 • **WB:** 1.1.3, 2.2.1, 2.2.3, 2.2.4	• See things in the mind's eye • Understand how systems work	• Get involved in the community and get others involved • Assist others • Find and use community resources and services	• **1:** 2.01.10 2.02.01, 2.02.02 • **3:** 2.06.02 • **4:** 2.06.03 • **6:** 2.02.01, 2.02.02 • **WB:** 2.06.01 • **RC:** 2.02.04	• **1:** 22, G1a, G16c • **2:** 9(d), 23(a, b), G14a • **3:** 42, G13b • **4:** 23(c), G9a • **5:** 9(d), 11(a, b, c) • **7:** 59 • **WB:** 17, 24 (a, b) • **RC:** 41
• Identify the business hours of places in the community • Distinguish U.S. coins and bills • **WB:** Identify methods of payment	• Interpret clock time • Use numbers 12 to 90 • Write the time using numbers • Count coins and bills • Read and understand price tags • Write dollar amounts on personal checks • Use addition and subtraction to calculate total costs	• **1:** 2.3.1, 6.0.1, 6.0.2 • **2:** 2.5.6, • **3:** 1.1.6, 6.1.1 • **4:** 1.8.1 • **5:** 2.1.8 • **6:** 4.2.1 • **WB:** 4.2.1, 4.4.1	• Understand how systems work	• Manage time and resources • Learn new skills	• **1:** 2.03.09, 2.04.01 • **2:** 2.02.02 • **3:** 2.04.06 • **4:** 2.01.05, 2.02.04 2.04.07 • **6:** 2.03.11 • **WB:** 2.04.07, 2.03.10 • **RC:** 2.04.08, 2.06.05	• **1:** 25, G13a • **2:** G16c • **3:** 30(a, b), G1a, G16a • **4:** G9a • **5:** 19 • **7:** 59 • **WB:** 57

CASAS, Florida, and LAUSD standards: Numbers in bold indicate lesson numbers. • **G**: Grammar Standard • **WB**: Workbook • **RC**: Online Teacher Resource Center

SCOPE AND SEQUENCE

LIFE SKILLS

UNIT	Listening and Speaking	Reading and Writing	Critical Thinking	Vocabulary	Grammar
Unit 4 **Calendars** *page 46*	• Talk about holidays • Talk about the weather • Talk about appointments • Make, cancel, and reschedule an appointment • Pron: Short *A* and long *A* • **WB:** Show surprise	• Read appointment cards • Read and write about holidays • Read a school calendar • Read about enrollment procedures • **WB:** Read a work schedule • **WB:** Read temperatures (Celsius and Fahrenheit)	• Classify information • Evaluate • Interpret information about appointments • Interpret information on a school calendar • Interpret enrollment procedures • **WB:** Interpret information on a work schedule	• Months of the year • Holidays • Ordinal numbers • Weather words	• Possessive nouns • Prepositions of time • Adjective + noun
Unit 5 **Clothing** *page 60*	• Ask for information in a store • Ask about sizes and prices • Describe clothing • Listen to a story • Give opinions about clothes • Return something to a store • Talk about appropriate clothing • Pron: Vowel sounds in *shoes* and *should*	• Add words to a Venn diagram • Describe clothes • Read store signs • Read price tags • Read a store receipt • Write a store receipt • Write a personal check • Read a story • Complete a story chart • Read an office memo • **WB:** Read clothing care labels	• Make inferences • Classify information • Sequence events • Predict • Summarize	• Clothing names • Colors • Department store people, places, and actions • Sizes • Prices • Descriptive words for clothing • **WB:** Clothing care words	• Present continuous, statements • Present continuous, questions • Demonstratives *this, that, these, those* • Articles: *a* and *an*
Unit 6 **Food** *page 74*	• Give opinions about foods • Ask for items in a grocery store • Describe food containers • Ask for price information • Listen to a recorded message • Talk about healthy food choices • Pron: Intonation in *yes/no* questions	• Write a shopping list • Read store flyers • Read store receipts • Read a recipe • Connect sentences with *and* • Write a recipe • **WB:** Spotlight: Writing: Recipes • **WB:** Read the USDA food pyramid	• Classify information • Make comparisons • Choose the best alternative • Sequence events	• Food • Descriptive words for food • Grocery store places, things, and actions • Food containers • **WB:** Restaurant occupations	• Simple Present, statements • Count and noncount nouns • *Want* and *need* • Simple Present, *Wh-* questions
Unit 7 **Families** *page 88*	• Talk about family members and responsibilities • Talk about personal interests and activities • Make telephone calls • Discuss family expenses • Give opinions about expenses • Pron: Linking consonant to vowel	• Make a family tree • Write about family responsibilities • Read family portraits and take notes • Write about family	• Classify information • Estimate	• Family members • Household activities • Park activities • Family expenses • **WB:** Types of identification	• Simple present of *have* • Simple present, *Yes/No* questions • Adverbs of frequency • Compound sentences with *and* and *but*

Civics Concepts	Math Skills	CASAS Life Skills Competencies	SCANS Competencies (Workplace)	EFF Content Standards	Florida	LAUSD
• Identify important holidays in the U.S.	• Use ordinal numbers • Read and write dates • Convert dates to numeric form • Interpret schedules • Understand appointment times and dates • **WB:** Convert Celsius and Fahrenheit temperatures	• **1:** 2.3.2, 2.3.3 • **2:** 0.1.2, 2.3.2, 2.3.4 • **3:** 0.1.2, 2.3.2, 2.3.4, 3.1.2 • **4:** 2.7.1 • **5:** 3.1.2 • **6:** 2.8.3 • **WB:** 1.1.5, 2.3.3, 4.1.6	• Problem solving • Self-management • Acquire and evaluate information	• Manage time and resources • Pass on values, ethics, and cultural heritage	• **2:** 2.04.01 • **3:** 2.01.05 • **4:** 2.01.03, 2.02.03 • **6:** 2.02.08 • **WB:** 2.02.05	• **1:** 28, G1a, G13a, G16c • **2:** 3, 26, G9c • **3:** 3, 27, G14c • **4:** 40, G12b • **7:** 59 • **WB:** 29, 55, 60
• Explore a department store • Interpret price tags and receipts • Recognize different occupations in the community	• Understand prices and sales receipts • Use multiplication and division to calculate totals	• **1:** 1.2.9, 1.3.7 • **2:** 1.2.7 • **3:** 1.2.1, 1.2.2, 1.6.4, 6.1.3 • **4:** 1.2.9 • **5:** 1.2.9, 1.3.3 • **6:** 4.4.1 • **WB:** 1.1.9, 1.3.3, 1.3.4, 1.7.2, 8.1.4, 8.2.4	• Creative thinking • Reasoning • See things in the mind's eye • Analyze and communicate information	• Provide for physical needs • Reflect on and reevaluate opinions and ideas	• **2:** 2.04.09 • **3:** 2.04.03 • **WB:** 2.04.03	• **1:** 33, G2 • **2:** 32, G2, G15a • **3:** 31, 34 • **4:** G10a • **7:** 59 • **WB:** 36
• Understand the food groups • Explore a grocery store • Interpret receipts • Understand healthy eating	• Use U.S. measurements: pounds, ounces, and cups • Compare prices • Budget for food • Calculate serving sizes • Read and write measurements for receipts	• **1:** 0.2.4, 1.2.8 • **2:** 1.2.7 • **3:** 1.1.7, 1.2.1 • **4:** 1.1.7 1.2.1, 1.2.2, 1.2.4 • **5:** 0.1.2, 1.2.1, 1.2.4 • **6:** 0.1.2, 2.6.4, 6.2.1, 6.2.3 • **WB:** 3.5.2, 4.1.8, 8.2.1, 8.2.2	• Decision making • Problem solving • See things in the mind's eye • Self-management • Use resources wisely • Teach others new skills • Acquire and evaluate information	• Find and use community resources and services • Find, interpret, and analyze diverse sources of information • Provide for physical needs • Communicate so that others understand	• **1:** 2.01.03 • **2:** 2.04.09 • **6:** 2.05.06	• **1:** 14 a, 35, G1c • **2:** 32, G9d • **3:** 31, G1b • **4:** G1c, G16c • **5:** 31, 36 • **7:** 59 • **WB:** 50, 51
• Discuss community-related activities	• Take messages that include telephone numbers • Create a household budget • Use addition and multiplication to calculate totals	• **1:** 0.1.2, 8.3.1 • **2:** 0.2.4, 8.2.1, 8.2.2, 8.2.3, 8.2.4 • **3:** 0.2.4 • **4:** 0.1.2, 8.3.1 • **5:** 2.1.7, 2.1.8 • **6:** 1.4.8, 3.4.2 • **WB:** 1.9.2, 2.5.5	• Self-management • Integrity and honesty • Use resources wisely • Acquire and evaluate information • Organize and maintain information	• Provide a nurturing home environment • Provide for physical needs • Teach children • Establish rules and expectations for children's behavior	• **1:** 2.02.07 • **4:** 2.02.07 • **5:** 2.01.07 • **6:** 2.06.04, 2.07.01 • **WB:** 2.02.08, 2.06.04 • **RC:** 2.01.06, 2.01.08	• **1:** 6, G1b • **2:** 12, 13, G1c, G16a • **3:** 12, 13, G15d • **4:** 6, G18 • **5:** 19, 20 • **7:** 59

CASAS, Florida, and LAUSD standards: Numbers in bold indicate lesson numbers. • **G**: Grammar Standard • **WB**: Workbook • **RC**: Online Teacher Resource Center

SCOPE AND SEQUENCE

LIFE SKILLS

UNIT	Listening and Speaking	Reading and Writing	Critical Thinking	Vocabulary	Grammar
Unit 8 **Health** *page 102*	• Talk about health problems • Discuss remedies • Listen to and practice 911 calls • Pron: Linking vowel to vowel with a *Y* or *W* sound	• Read opinion paragraphs • Read bar graphs • Indent a paragraph • Write an opinion paragraph • Draw a bar graph • **WB:** Spotlight: Writing: Opinions	• Classify information • Make inferences • Analyze arguments • Make decisions	• Parts of the body • Health problems • Remedies • **WB:** Hygiene words • **WB:** Emergency services	• *Can* and *can't* for ability • Questions with *can* • *Should* and *shouldn't* for advice • Object pronouns
Unit 9 **House and Home** *page 116*	• Describe things in a house • Talk about accidents in the home • Ask for housing information • Pron: Stress in compound nouns • **WB:** Talk about safety procedures at work • **WB:** Talk about emergency evacuation procedures • **WB:** Ask for the next step	• Write a comparison of two houses • Read bar graphs • Read classified ads • Read bills • Write personal checks • **WB:** Write about a time you got hurt	• Compare and contrast • Choose the best alternative • Classify information • Make decisions	• Areas of a house • Household furniture and other items • Features of a house • Types of housing • Classified ad abbreviations • Utility bills • **WB:** Workplace protective equipment	• Adjective order • Simple past of *be* • Simple past of regular verbs • *Can, may* and *would like* for requests and offers
Unit 10 **Work** *page 130*	• Respond to job ads • Listen to a job interview • Give reasons • Pron: Past tense endings • **WB:** Talk about goals	• Read and write help wanted ads • Read a success story • Write a story • Read for specific information • Complete job applications • Complete an idea list • **WB:** Read a job evaluation • **WB:** Spotlight: Writing: Past tense stories	• Classify information • Reason • Sequence events	• Occupations and skills • Help wanted ad abbreviations • Work experience • **WB:** Job requirements	• Simple past of irregular verbs • Future with *will* • Adverbs of manner • Future with *be going to*

CORRELATIONS TO STANDARDS

Civics Concepts	Math Skills	CASAS Life Skills Competencies	SCANS Competencies (Workplace)	EFF Content Standards	Florida	LAUSD
• Explore a health clinic • Understand when to call 911 • Explore a hospital • **WB:** Access emergency services	• Use U.S. measurements: gallons, quarts, pints, cups and ounces • Interpret bar graphs	• **1:** 3.6.1, 3.6.3 • **2:** 3.1.3, 3.6.3 • **3:** 0.1.7, 3.1.3, 3.6.4 • **4:** 3.3.1, 3.3.2, 3.3.4 • **5:** 2.1.2, 2.5.1, 3.6.3 • **6:** 0.1.3, 1.1.4, 1.1.7, 3.4.1, 6.1.3 • **WB:** 2.5.3, 3.1.3, 3.5.5, 8.1.1	• Reasoning • See things in the mind's eye • Integrity and honesty • Organize and maintain information	• Provide for physical needs • Find and use community resources and services • Exercise human and legal rights and civic responsibilities • Help self and others	• **1:** 2.05.01 • **2:** 2.05.01, 2.05.02 • **3:** 2.05.02 • **4:** 2.05.04, **WB:** 2.07.03 • **5:** 2.01.09, 2.05.01, 2.05.02, 2.07.02 • **6:** 2.04.02, 2.07.03 • **WB:** 2.01.09, 2.02.01, 2.02.02, 2.05.03, 2.05.05, 2.02.09	• **1:** 43, G6 • **2:** 44, G6, G16a • **3:** 46 • **4:** 45, G11 (a, b) • **5:** 21 • **6:** 48, 49 • **7:** 59
• Recognize different types of housing in a community • Use classified ads as a source of community information **WB:** Understand emergency evacuation procedures	• Interpret bar graphs • Compare rent prices for apartments and houses • Interpret and pay bills	• **1:** 1.4.1, 1.4.8 • **2:** 1.4.1 • **3:** 6.7.2 • **4:** 1.4.1, 1.4.2 • **5:** 1.4.2 • **6:** 1.4.4, 1.5.3 • **WB:** 0.1.3, 1.1.3, 2.2.1, 3.4.2, 4.3.2, 4.3.3	• Decision making • See things in the mind's eye • Acquire and evaluate information	• Find, interpret, and analyze diverse sources of information • Provide for physical needs • Find and use community resources and services	• **4:** 2.04.04 • **6:** 2.04.05 • **WB:** 2.03.08, 2.07.02 • **RC:** 2.02.06	• **1:** 38, G12b • **2:** 38, G4a • **4:** G4b • **4:** 10, 39, G7 • **5:** 38, 39, G20 • **7:** 59 • **WB:** 47, 48
• Use help wanted ads as a source of community information • Recognize some dos and don'ts of interviewing	• Solve word problems • Understand hourly wages • Use addition and multiplication to calculate totals	• **1:** 4.1.8 • **2:** 4.1.3 • **3:** 0.1.1, 4.1.5, 4.1.7 • **5:** 4.1.5, 4.1.7 • **6:** 4.1.2, 6.1.5 • **WB:** 4.4.1, 4.4.2, 4.4.3, 4.4.4, 4.4.5, 4.4.6, 4.6.1, 4.6.5, 4.7.3, 7.1.1, 7.1.2, 7.1.3, 7.1.4, 8.3.1	• Problem solving • Self-esteem • Integrity and honesty • Acquire and evaluate information • Analyze and communicate information • Work within the system	• Find and get a job • Plan and renew career goals • Find, interpret, and analyze diverse sources of information	• **2:** 2.03.01, 2.03.05, 2.03.07 • **3:** 2.01.04, 2.03.02, 2.03.04 • **5:** 2.03.04, 2.03.06 • **6:** 2.01.05, 2.03.03 • **WB:** 2.03.06, 2.03.10, 2.03.12, 2.03.13, 2.03.14, 2.03.15 • **RC:** 2.03.16	• **1:** 50, 51, G4 (b, c) • **4:** G3 • **2:** 52 • **3:** 54 • **5:** 54, 59 • **RC:** 53, 56

CASAS, Florida, and LAUSD standards: Numbers in bold indicate lesson numbers. • **G:** Grammar Standard • **WB:** Workbook • **RC:** Online Teacher Resource Center

TO THE TEACHER

All-Star Second Edition is a four-level, standards-based series for English learners featuring a picture-dictionary approach to vocabulary building. "Big picture" scenes in each unit provide springboards to a wealth of activities developing all of the language skills.

An accessible and predictable sequence of lessons in each unit systematically builds language and critical thinking skills around life-skill topics. *All-Star* presents family, work, and community topics in each unit and provides alternate application lessons in its workbooks, giving teachers the flexibility to customize the series for a variety of student needs and curricular objectives. *All-Star* is tightly correlated to all of the updated major national and state standards for adult instruction.

New to the Second Edition

- **Updated content** provides full coverage of all major *revised* standards including CASAS, Florida, LAUSD, EFF, and Texas.
- **NEW comprehensive, carefully sequenced grammar program** connects target grammar to the content to enrich learning and provide full coverage of grammar standards.
- **NEW robust listening program** addresses the latest CASAS standards and prepares students for the types of listening items on CASAS tests.
- **NEW Work-Out CD-ROM with complete student audio** provides a fun, rich environment with over 25 hours of interactive learning and the entire *All-Star Second Edition* student audio program in downloadable MP3 files.
- **NEW Teacher Resource Center** offers downloadable and printable Study Guides and Learner Persistence Worksheets, EZ-Tests, Big Picture PowerPoint Slides, full Teacher Audio for Tests in downloadable MP3 files, and other materials to support teaching.
- **NEW Interactive Correlations Chart** allows teachers to easily cross-reference standards with Student Book, Workbook, and Study Guide pages.

Hallmark *All-Star* Features

- Dynamic Big Picture scenes present life-skills vocabulary and provide lively contexts for activities and discussions that promote all-skills language development.
- Predictable sequence of seven two-page lessons in each unit reduces prep time for teachers and helps students get comfortable with the format of each lesson.
- Flexible structure, with application lessons addressing family, work, and community topics in both the Student Book and Workbook, allows teachers to customize each unit to meet a variety of student needs and curricular objectives.
- Comprehensive coverage of key standards, such as CASAS, Florida, LAUSD, EFF, and Texas, prepares students to master a broad range of critical competencies.

- Multiple assessment measures like CASAS-style tests and performance-based assessment offer a variety of options for monitoring and assessing learner progress.

The Complete *All-Star* Program

- The **Student Book** features ten 14-page units that integrate listening, speaking, reading, writing, grammar, math, and pronunciation skills with life-skills topics, critical thinking activities, and civics concepts.
- The **Student Work-Out CD-ROM with full student audio** extends the learning goals of each Student Book unit with interactive activities that build vocabulary, listening, reading, writing, and test-taking skills. The CD-ROM also includes the full Student Book audio program.
- The **Teacher's Edition with Tests** includes:
  - Step-by-step procedural notes for each Student Book activity
  - Notes on teaching the Target Grammar Pages
  - Expansion activities addressing multi-level classes, literacy, and students that need to be challenged
  - Culture, Grammar, and Pronunciation Notes
  - Two-page written test for each unit (Note: Listening passages for the tests are available on the Teacher Audio with Testing CD and on the Online Teacher Resource Center.)
  - Audio scripts for all audio program materials
  - Answer keys for Student Book, Workbook, and Tests
- The **Workbook** includes supplementary practice activities correlated to the Student Book. As a bonus feature, the Workbook also includes two alternate application lessons per unit that address the learner's role as a worker, family member, and/or community member. These lessons may be used in addition to, or as substitutes for, the application lessons found in Lesson 6 of each Student Book unit.
- The **Teacher Audio with Testing CD** contains recordings for all listening activities in the Student Book as well as the listening passages for each unit test.
- The **Online Teacher Resource Center** provides teachers with the tools to set goals for students, customize classroom teaching, and better measure student success. It includes:
  - EZ-Tests that allow teachers to create customized online tests
  - An Interactive Correlations Chart that allows teachers to easily cross-reference standards with Student Book, Workbook, and Study Guide pages
  - Big Picture PowerPoint slides that present the Student Book Big Picture scenes
  - A Learner Persistence Kit that sets and tracks student achievement goals
  - A Post-Testing Study Guide that moves students toward mastery and tracks their progress using the reproducible Study Guide Worksheets
  - Downloadable MP3 files for the Testing audio program

Overview of the *All-Star Second Edition* Program

UNIT STRUCTURE

The *Welcome to All-Star Second Edition* guide on pages xiv–xix offers teachers and administrators a visual tour of one Student Book unit and highlights the exciting new features of the Second Edition.

All-Star Second Edition is designed to maximize flexibility. Each unit has the following sequence of seven two-page lessons:

- Lesson 1: Vocabulary
- Lesson 2: Vocabulary in Action
- Lesson 3: Talk about It
- Lesson 4: Reading and Writing
- Lesson 5: Conversations
- Lesson 6: Application
- Lesson 7: Review and Assessment

Each unit introduces several grammar points. A Target Grammar icon

Target Grammar
Possessive nouns   *page xxx*

in the lessons refers teachers and student to the Target Grammar Pages at the back of the book where they can find explanations of the grammar points and contextualized practice.

SPECIAL FEATURES OF EACH UNIT

- **Target Grammar Pages:** Throughout each unit, students are directed to the Target Grammar Pages in the back of the book, where the grammar point they have been exposed to in the lesson is presented and practiced in manageable chunks. Students learn the target grammar structure with clear charts, meaningful examples, and abundant practice activities.

  This approach gives teachers the flexibility to introduce grammar in any of several ways:
  1) At the beginning of a lesson
  2) At the point in the lesson where the grammar appears in context
  3) As a follow-up to the lesson

- **CASAS Listening:** Each unit has at least two activities that simulate the CASAS listening experience.

- **Pronunciation.** The introductory activity in Lesson 5 (Conversation) of each unit is Pronunciation. This special feature has two major goals: (1) helping students hear and produce specific sounds, words, and minimal pairs of words so they become better listeners and speakers; and (2) addressing issues of stress, rhythm, and intonation so that the students' spoken English becomes more comprehensible.

- **Window on Math.** Learning basic math skills is critically important for success in school, on the job, and at home. As such, national and state standards for adult education mandate instruction in basic math skills. In each unit, a box called Window on Math is dedicated to helping students develop the functional numeracy skills they need for basic math work.

TWO-PAGE LESSON FORMAT

The lessons in *All-Star* are designed as two-page spreads. Lessons 1–4 follow an innovative format with a list of activities on the left-hand page of the spread and picture dictionary visuals supporting these activities on the right hand page. The list of activities, entitled Things to Do, allows students and teachers to take full advantage of the visuals in each lesson, enabling students to achieve a variety of learning goals.

"BIG PICTURE" SCENES

Each unit includes one "big picture" scene in either Lesson 2 or Lesson 3. This scene is the visual centerpiece of each unit, and serves as a springboard to a variety of activities in the Student Book, Teacher's Edition, and Work-Out CD-ROM. In the Student Book, the "big picture" scene introduces key vocabulary and serves as a prompt for classroom discussion. The scenes feature characters with distinct personalities for students to enjoy, respond to, and talk about. There are also surprising and fun elements for students to discover in each scene.

The Teacher's Edition includes a variety of all-skills "Big Picture Expansion" activities that are tied to the Student Book scenes. For each unit, these expansion activities address listening, speaking, reading, writing, and grammar skills development, and allow teachers to customize their instruction to meet the language learning needs of each group of students.

CIVICS CONCEPTS

Many institutions focus direct attention on the importance of civics instruction for English language learners. Civics instruction encourages students to become active and informed community members. Throughout each *All-Star* unit, students and teachers will encounter activities that introduce civics concepts and encourage community involvement. In addition, Application lessons provide activities that help students develop in their roles as workers, parents, and citizens. Those lessons targeting the students' role as citizen encourage learners to become more active and informed members of their communities.

CASAS, SCANS, EFF, FLORIDA, TEXAS, LAUSD, AND OTHER STANDARDS

Teachers and administrators benchmark student progress against national and/or state standards for adult instruction. With this in mind, *All-Star* carefully integrates instructional elements from a wide range of revised standards including CASAS, SCANS, EFF, LAUSD, Texas, and the Florida Adult ESOL Standards. Unit-by-unit correlations of these standards appear in the scope and sequence in the front of this book and in the Online Teacher Resource Center. Here is a brief overview of our approach to meeting the key national, state, and district standards.

- **CASAS.** Many U.S. states, including California, tie funding for adult education programs to student performance on the Comprehensive Adult Student Assessment System (CASAS). The CASAS (www.casas.org) competencies identify more than 300 essential skills that adults need in order to succeed in the classroom, workplace, and community. Examples of these skills

To the Teacher

include identifying or using appropriate nonverbal behavior in a variety of settings, responding appropriately to common personal information questions, and comparing price or quality to determine the best buys. *All-Star* comprehensively integrates all of the CASAS Life Skill Competencies throughout the four levels of the series.

- **SCANS.** Developed by the United States Department of Labor, SCANS is an acronym for the Secretary's Commission on Achieving Necessary Skills (wdr.doleta.gov/SCANS/). SCANS competencies are workplace skills that help people compete more effectively in today's global economy. The following are examples of SCANS competencies: works well with others, acquires and evaluates information, and teaches others new skills. A variety of SCANS competencies is threaded throughout the activities in each unit of *All-Star*. The incorporation of these competencies recognizes both the intrinsic importance of teaching workplace skills and the fact that many adult students are already working members of their communities.

- **EFF.** Equipped for the Future (EFF) is a set of standards for adult literacy and lifelong learning developed by The National Institute for Literacy (www.nifl.gov). The organizing principle of EFF is that adults assume responsibilities in three major areas of life—as workers, as parents, and as citizens. These three areas of focus are called "role maps" in the EFF documentation. In the parent role map, for example, EFF highlights these and other responsibilities: participating in children's formal education and forming and maintaining supportive family relationships. *All-Star* addresses all three of the EFF role maps in its *Application* lessons.

NUMBER OF HOURS OF INSTRUCTION

The *All-Star* program has been designed to accommodate the needs of adult classes with 70–180 hours of classroom instruction. Here are three recommended ways in which various components in the *All-Star* program can be combined to meet student and teacher needs.

- **70–100 hours.** Teachers are encouraged to work through all of the Student Book materials. Teachers should also look to the Teacher's Edition for teaching suggestions and testing materials as necessary. Students are encouraged to "Plug in and practice" at home with the Work-Out CD-ROM for each unit.
  Time per unit: 7–10 hours

- **100–140 hours.** In addition to working through all of the Student Book materials, teachers are encouraged to incorporate the Workbook and Work-Out CD-ROM activities for supplementary practice. Students are encouraged to "Plug in and practice" at home with the Work-Out CD-ROM for each unit.
  Time per unit: 10–14 hours

- **140–180 hours.** Teachers and students working in an intensive instructional setting can take advantage of the wealth of expansion activities threaded through the Teacher's Edition to supplement the Student Book, Workbook, and Work-Out CD-ROM materials. Students are encouraged to "Plug in and practice" at home with the Work-Out CD-ROM for each unit.
  Time per unit: 14–18 hours.

ASSESSMENT

The *All-Star* program offers teachers, students and administrators the following wealth of resources for monitoring and assessing student progress and achievement:

- **Standardized testing formats.** *All-Star* is correlated to the CASAS competencies and many other national and state standards for adult learning. Students have the opportunity to practice answering CASAS-style listening questions in Lesson 7 of each unit. Students practice with the same item types and bubble-in answer sheets they encounter on CASAS and other standardized tests. Student also practice CASAS-style listening items in the Work-Out CD-ROM Listening and Practice Test sections.

- **Achievement tests.** The *All-Star Teacher's Edition* includes end-of-unit tests. These paper-and-pencil tests help students demonstrate how well they have learned the instructional content of the unit. Adult learners often show incremental increases in learning that are not always measured on the standardized tests. The achievement tests may demonstrate learning even in a short amount of instructional time. Twenty percent of each test includes questions that encourage students to apply more academic skills such as determining meaning from context, making inferences, and understanding main ideas. Practice with these question types will help prepare students who may want to enroll in academic classes.

- **EZ Test Online.** *All-Star's* online test generator provides a databank of assessment items from which instructors can create customized tests within minutes. The EZ Test Online assessment materials are available at www.eztestonline.com. For EZ Test tutorials, go to http://mpss.mhhe.com/eztest/eztotutorials.php.

- **Performance-based assessment.** *All-Star* provides several ways to measure students' performance on productive tasks, including the Spotlight: Writing located in the Workbook in the second edition. In addition, the Teacher's Edition suggests writing and speaking prompts that teachers can use for performance-based assessment. These prompts derive from the "big picture" scene in each unit, which provides rich visual input as the basis for the speaking and writing tasks asked of the students.

- **Portfolio assessment.** A portfolio is a collection of student work that can be used to show progress. Examples of work that the instructor or the student may submit in the portfolio include writing samples, audio and video recordings, or projects. Every Student Book unit includes several activities that require critical thinking and small-group project work. These can be included in a student's portfolio.

- **Self-assessment.** Self-assessment is an important part of the overall assessment picture, as it promotes student involvement and commitment to the learning process. When encouraged to assess themselves, students take more control of their learning and are better able to connect the instructional content with their own goals. The Student Book includes *Learning Logs* at the end of each unit, which allow students to check off the vocabulary they have learned and the skills they feel they have acquired. In the Workbook, students complete the Practice Test Performance Record on the inside back cover.

- **Other linguistic and nonlinguistic outcomes.** Traditional testing often does not account for the progress made by adult learners with limited educational experience or low literacy levels. Such learners tend to take longer to make smaller language gains, so the gains they make in other areas are often more significant. These gains may be in areas such as self-esteem, goal clarification, learning skills, access to employment, community involvement and further academic studies. The SCANS and EFF standards identify areas of student growth that are not necessarily language based. *All-Star* is correlated with both SCANS and EFF standards. Like the Student Book, the Workbook includes activities that provide documentation that can be added to a student portfolio.

About the author and series consultants

Linda Lee is lead author on the *All-Star* series. Linda has taught ESL/ELT in the United States, Iran, and China, and has authored or co-authored a variety of successful textbook series for English learners. As a classroom instructor, Linda's most satisfying teaching experiences have been with adult ESL students at Roxbury Community College in Boston, Massachusetts.

Grace Tanaka is professor and coordinator of ESL at the Santa Ana College School of Continuing Education in Santa Ana, California, which serves more than 20,000 students per year. She is also a textbook co-author and series consultant. Grace has 25 years of teaching experience in both credit and non-credit ESL programs.

Shirley Velasco is principal at Miami Beach Adult and Community Education Center in Miami Beach, Florida. She has been a classroom instructor and administrator for the past 28 years. Shirley has created a large adult ESL program based on a curriculum she helped develop to implement state/national ESL standards.

Welcome to *All-Star*
Second Edition

All-Star is a four-level series featuring a "big picture" approach to meeting adult standards that systematically builds language and math skills around life-skill topics.

Complete Standards Coverage Using the "Big Picture" Approach

ACCESSIBLE, TWO-PAGE LESSON FORMAT follows an innovative layout with a list of activities labeled "Things to Do" on the left and picture-dictionary visuals on the right.

COMPREHENSIVE COVERAGE OF REVISED KEY STANDARDS, such as CASAS, Florida, Texas, LAUSD, and EFF prepares students to master critical competencies.

PREDICTABLE UNIT STRUCTURE includes the same logical sequence of seven two-page lessons in each unit.

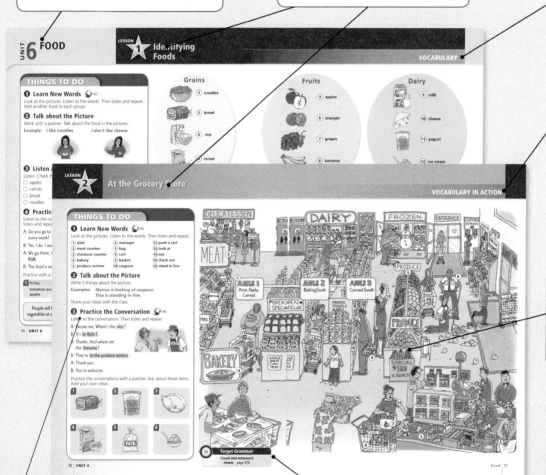

"BIG PICTURE" SCENES are springboards to the lesson and to a wealth of all-skills expansion activities in the Teacher's Edition and NEW Work-Out CD-ROM.

STRUCTURED SPEAKING ACTIVITIES invite students to discuss the picture dictionary scene, simulate real-life conversations, and express their thoughts and opinions.

NEW

TARGET GRAMMAR points students to the Target Grammar Pages where they find manageable chunks of grammar with clear examples and plentiful follow up activities.

NEW Comprehensive Grammar Program

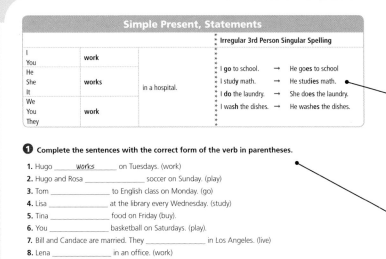

CAREFULLY SEQUENCED GRAMMAR covers grammar standards and introduces, builds on, and practices grammar throughout the book and series.

GRAMMAR CHARTS with clear presentations and examples make it easy to learn the target grammar.

CONTEXTUALIZED GRAMMAR PRACTICE helps students internalize the grammar.

UNIT 6 FOOD

LESSON 1 — Simple Present, Statements *pages 74–75*

Simple Present, Statements

			Irregular 3rd Person Singular Spelling	
I / You	work		I **go** to school. → He **goes** to school	
He / She / It	works	in a hospital.	I **study** math. → He **studies** math.	
We / You / They	work		I **do** the laundry. → She **does** the laundry.	
			I **wash** the dishes. → He **washes** the dishes.	

❶ Complete the sentences with the correct form of the verb in parentheses.

1. Hugo _____works_____ on Tuesdays. (work)
2. Hugo and Rosa _____ soccer on Sunday. (play)
3. Tom _____ to English class on Monday. (go)
4. Lisa _____ at the library every Wednesday. (study)
5. Tina _____ food on Friday (buy).
6. You _____ basketball on Saturdays. (play).
7. Bill and Candace are married. They _____ in Los Angeles. (live)
8. Lena _____ in an office. (work)
9. He _____ work at 6:00 P.M. (leave)
10. They _____ work in the morning. (leave)

NEW Work-Out CD-ROM with Interactive Activities and Complete Student Audio

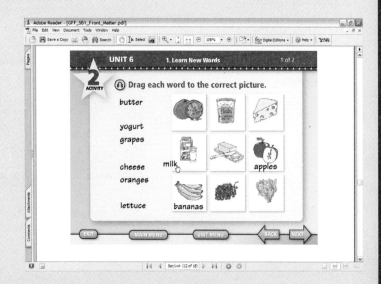

- Over 25 hours of listening, reading, writing, and grammar activities
- Voice record activities
- Entire student audio program MP3s for download

Integrated Skills with Enhanced Listening

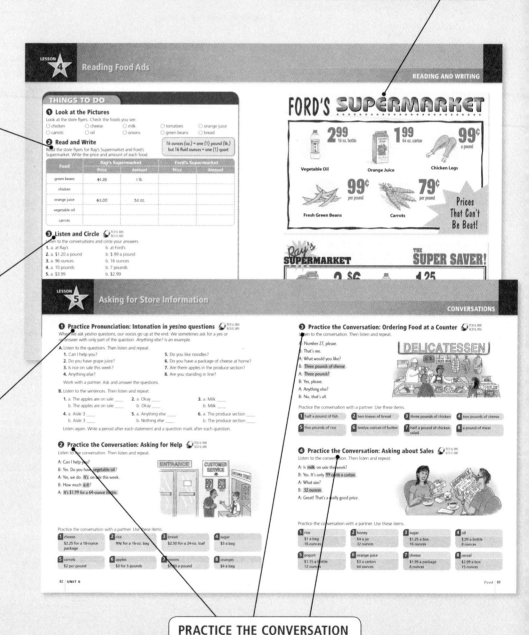

Real World Applications

APPLICATION LESSON IN EACH UNIT focuses on developing the students' roles in life as workers, parents, and citizens.

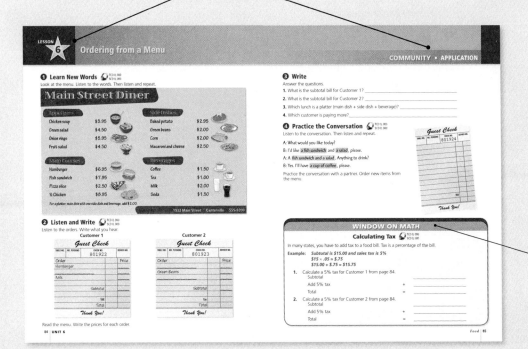

WINDOWS ON MATH help students build numeracy skills for basic math work.

ALTERNATE APPLICATION LESSONS IN THE WORKBOOK provide a flexible approach to addressing family, work, and community topics.

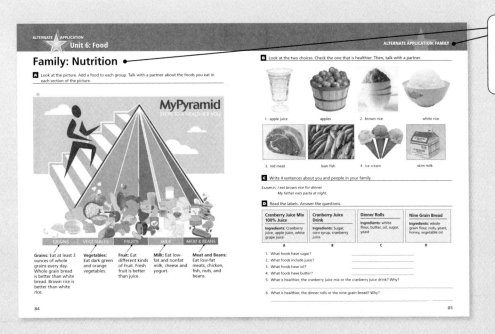

Multiple Opportunities for Assessment

CASAS LISTENING REVIEW helps teachers assess listening comprehension, while giving students practice with the item types and answer sheets they encounter on standardized tests.

GRAMMAR REVIEW provides an opportunity to assess and review the unit grammar point.

LISTENING DICTATION provides an opportunity to assess listening and writing.

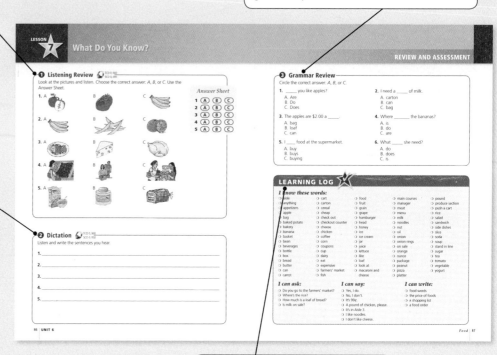

LEARNING LOGS ask students to catalog the vocabulary, grammar, and life skills they have learned, and determine which areas they need to review.

WORKBOOK AND NEW WORK-OUT CD-ROM PRACTICE TESTS provide additional practice.

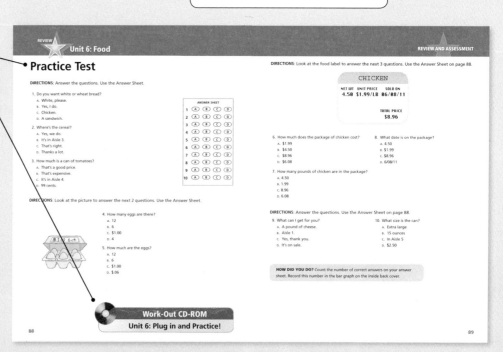

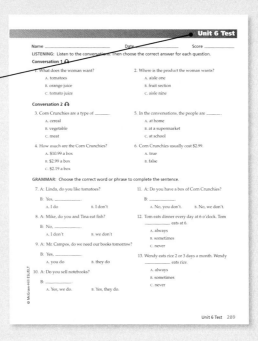

UNIT TEST in the Teacher's Edition rounds out the assessment program.

NEW Online Teacher Resource Center

- EZ Test Online bank of 500+ test questions for teachers to create customized tests.
- Study Guide reproducible worksheets support a portfolio-based approach to assessment.
- Persistence Kit includes reproducible worksheets that promote student goal setting and achievement.
- Interactive Correlations Chart allows teachers easy and immediate access to standards coverage in the *All-Star Second Edition* program.

MEETING YOUR CLASSMATES

Introductions

❶ Practice the Conversation 002

Listen to the conversation. Then listen and repeat.

A: Hello. My name is Anna.

B: Hi. I'm Tom.

A: Nice to meet you, Tom.

B: Nice to meet you, too.

Practice the conversation with 3 classmates.

❷ Say the Alphabet 003

Listen to the letters. Then listen and repeat.

A a	B b	C c	D d
E e	F f	G g	H h
I i	J j	K k	L l
M m	N n	O o	P p
Q q	R r	S s	T t
U u	V v	W w	X x
Y y	Z z		

❸ Practice the Conversation 004

Listen to the conversation. Then listen and repeat.

A: What's your first name?

B: Sue .

A: What's your last name?

B: Chavez .

A: How do you spell that?

B: C-h-a-v-e-z .

Ask 6 classmates. Write their answers below.

FIRST NAME (GIVEN NAME)	LAST NAME (FAMILY NAME)
Sue	Chavez

❹ Write

Read Sue's name tag. Make a name tag for yourself.

Hi. My name is

Sue Chavez

Hi. My name is

_____

THINGS TO DO

❶ Find the Countries 005

Look at the map. Listen to the words. Then listen and repeat.
Write the name of one more country on the map.

❷ Listen and Circle 006

Listen to the conversation. Circle the correct name.

1. Alex   Tam   Amine
2. Alex   Tam   Amine
3. Alex   Tam   Amine

❸ Ask Questions 007

Listen to the conversation. Then listen and repeat.

A: What's your name?

B: My name is Victor .

A: How do you spell that?

B: V-I-C-T-O-R .

A: Where are you from?

B: I'm from Mexico .

A: Mexico ? That's interesting.

Ask 4 classmates: What's your name? How do you spell that?
Where are you from? Write their answers below.

What's your name?	Where are you from?
Victor	Mexico

❹ Write

Write about 4 classmates.

Example: *Victor is from Mexico.*

① Canada

② the United States

④ Haiti

③ Mexico

⑤ El Salvador

⑥ Colombia

⑦ Brazil

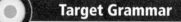
Target Grammar

Simple present of *be*,
statements   *page 144*

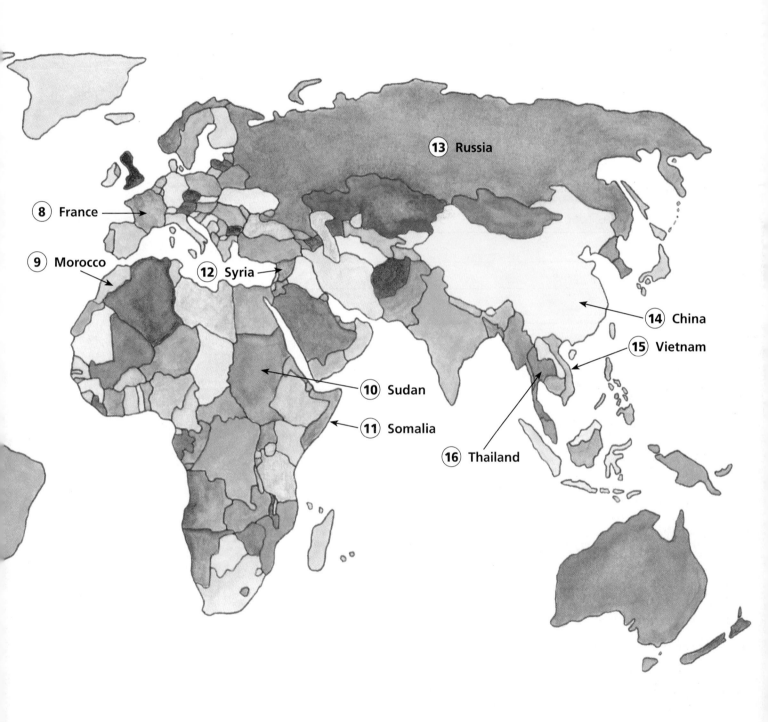

8. France
9. Morocco
10. Sudan
11. Somalia
12. Syria
13. Russia
14. China
15. Vietnam
16. Thailand

Work-Out CD-ROM

Unit 1: Plug in and practice!

In the Classroom

THINGS TO DO

❶ Learn New Words 🎧 008

Look at the picture. Listen to the words. Then listen and repeat.

① teacher ⑥ eraser ⑪ pen ⑮ floor
② wall ⑦ map ⑫ pencil ⑯ chair
③ clock ⑧ desk ⑬ piece of ⑰ computer
④ door ⑨ table   paper ⑱ student
⑤ board ⑩ notebook ⑭ book ⑲ bookbag

❷ Write

What's in your classroom? Write 5 things.

_____clock_____ _____
_____ _____
_____ _____

Tell your 5 things to the class.

❸ Listen and Complete 🎧 009

Listen. Complete the sentences. Listen again to check your answers.

1. The _____ is on the table.
2. The _____ is on the wall.
3. The _____ is on the floor.
4. The _____ is on the desk.
5. The _____ is on the table.

❹ Ask Questions

Work with a partner. Ask and answer questions about the picture.

A: Where's the map ?

B: It's on the wall .

Ask about these things.

 1   2   3   4

Use these places.

wall   floor   table   desk

Target Grammar

Prepositions of place   *page 147*

Understanding Classroom Instructions

THINGS TO DO

❶ Learn New Words 010

Look at the pictures. Listen to the instructions. Then listen and repeat.

❷ Follow Instructions

Work with a partner. Take turns giving 5 instructions.

Example: *Raise your hand.*

❸ Write

Write your own instructions. Then give one instruction to the class.

1. Say _____hello._____

2. Write _____

3. Open _____

4. Close _____

5. Go to _____

❹ Complete the Chart

Write words in the chart.

Things you open and close	Things you take out	Things you read
door		

① Read page 10.

⑦ Write your name.

⑬ Stand up.

(2) **Listen to the words.**

(3) **Repeat the words.**

(4) **Say computer.**

(5) **Ask a partner.**

(6) **Circle letter b.**

(8) **Practice the conversation with a partner.**

(9) **Take out a piece of paper.**

(10) **Open your book.**

(11) **Close the window.**

(12) **Raise your hand.**

(14) **Sit down.**

(15) **Go to the board.**

WINDOW ON MATH

Numbers 0 to 14 🎧 011

A Listen to the numbers. Then listen and repeat.

0	1	2	3	4
zero	one	two	three	four
5	6	7	8	9
five	six	seven	eight	nine
10	11	12	13	14
ten	eleven	twelve	thirteen	fourteen

B Listen to the conversation. Then listen and repeat.

A: Open your book to page 5.

B: Which page?

A: Page 5.

Practice the conversation with a partner. Use different numbers.

⊙ **Target Grammar**

Singular and plural nouns
page 148

Reporting Personal Information

THINGS TO DO

❶ Learn New Words 🎧 012

Look at the form on page 11. Listen to the words. Then listen and repeat.

❷ Read and Write

Read the form. Complete the sentences below.

Paul's ___last name___ is Bridges. His _____
        ①   ②

is Richard. His _____ is 1640 East Flower Street in
               ③

Los Angeles, California. His _____ is 91012.
                         ④

His _____ is (310) 555-5678. His
                ⑤

_____ is Sacramento. His _____
     ⑥   ⑦

is 11/12/82. His _____ is teacher.
                  ⑧

❸ Complete the Form

Work with a partner. Ask questions. Write your partner's answers on the form.

Example: *What's your first name?*

WRITING TIP
- Use periods for abbreviations (Street = St.).
- Use a comma between the city and state (Sacramento, CA).

Personal Information Form

(PLEASE PRINT)

Name _____
        First   Middle   Last

Address _____
         Street   City   State   Zip Code

Telephone Number _____
                         Area Code

Birthplace _____ Birthdate _____

Gender: ☐ Male ☐ Female   Marital Status: ☐ Single ☐ Married ☐ Divorced

Occupation _____

Personal Information Form

(1) (PLEASE PRINT)

Name __Paul__   __Richard__   __Bridges__
First   (3)   Middle   (4)   Last   (5)

(2) Address __1640 East Flower Street, LosAngeles,__   __CA__ __91012__ (6)
                  Street   City   State   Zip Code

(7)
Telephone Number ___(310) 555-5678___
(8)   Area Code

(9)
Birthplace __Sacramento, CA, U.S.__   (10) Birthdate __11/12/82__

(11)   (12)   (13)   (14)   (15)   (16)   (17)
Gender: ☑ Male   ☐ Female   Marital Status: ☐ Single   ☑ Married   ☐ Divorced

(18)
Occupation __Teacher__

Target Grammar

Possessive adjectives   *page 149*

LESSON 5

Greeting People

❶ Practice Pronunciation: Long *I* and Long *E* 013

> To say the long *I* sound, open your mouth wide from top to bottom.
> To say the long *E* sound, make a big smile.

A. Listen to the words. Then listen and repeat.

1. I	**4.** m<u>e</u>	**7.** m<u>y</u>	**10.** str<u>ee</u>t	**13.** wr<u>i</u>te
2. f<u>i</u>ne	**5.** m<u>ee</u>t	**8.** thr<u>ee</u>	**11.** Ch<u>i</u>na	**14.** n<u>i</u>ce
3. s<u>ee</u>	**6.** h<u>i</u>	**9.** h<u>e</u>	**12.** w<u>e</u>	**15.** r<u>ea</u>d

B. Write the words from Activity A in the correct place.

Sounds like *I*		Sounds like *E*	
I	_____	see	_____
fine	_____	me	_____
_____	_____	_____	_____
_____	_____	_____	_____
_____	_____	_____	_____

C. Listen and circle the word you hear. 014

1. I	E	**3.** hi	he	**5.** tie	T	**7.** why	we
2. my	me	**4.** bye	be	**6.** nice	niece	**8.** write	read

❷ Practice the Conversation: Greeting Someone 015

Listen to the conversation. Then listen and repeat.

A: Hello. I'm Mr. Campos.

B: Nice to meet you, Mr. Campos. I'm Ms. Jones.

A: Nice to meet you.

Mr. Campos

Ms. Jones

Practice the conversation with a partner. Use these items.

1 Hi.
Mrs. Lee

2 Hello.
Ms. Lopez

3 Hello.
Ms. Kim

4 How do you do?
Mrs. Bridges

5 Hi.
Mr. Adams

6 How do you do?
Mr. Thomas

> Mr. = a single or married male
> Ms. = a single or married female
> Mrs. = a married female

❸ Practice the Conversation: Introducing Someone 🎧 016

Listen to the conversation. Then listen and repeat.

A: Hi, John. How are you?

B: Fine , thanks. And you?

A: I'm fine. John, this is my friend Gina.

B: Hi, Gina. Nice to meet you.

Practice the conversation with a partner. Use these items.

1 Terrific	**2** Couldn't be better	**3** Pretty good	**4** Okay
I want to introduce you to	this is	I'd like you to meet	I want you to meet

5 Great	**6** Good	**7** Fine	**8** Not bad
I want you to meet	I'd like you to meet	I want to introduce you to	this is

❹ Practice the Conversation: Saying Good-bye 🎧 017

Listen to the conversation. Then listen and repeat.

A: Well, we have to go.

B. Yeah, me too.

A: Good-bye, John.

B: Bye, David. Have a nice day.

A: You too.

Practice the conversation with a partner. Use these items.

1 See you later.	**2** Nice to see you.	**3** Have a great day.	**4** Have a good day.	**5** See you soon.
Have a nice day.	Nice to see you, too.	Okay, you too.	Thanks, you too.	Take care.

Looking at Job Ads

❶ Learn New Words 018

Look at the pictures. Listen to the words. Then listen and repeat.

① Joan Cho is a <u>dentist</u>.

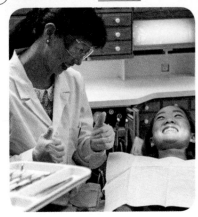

② Lori Fisher is a <u>bus driver</u>.

③ Ken Parker is a <u>pharmacist</u>.

④ Jeff Lambert is a <u>doctor</u>.

⑤ Paula Cruz is a <u>salesclerk</u>.

⑥ Steven Morales is a <u>machinist</u>.

⑦ Meg Lewis is a <u>police officer</u>.

⑧ Leo Brunov is a <u>nurse</u>.

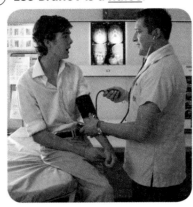

⑨ Amy Sherman is a <u>cashier</u>.

❷ Ask Questions

Work with a partner. Ask about the people in the pictures.

Example: A: What is Joan's occupation?
            B: She is a dentist.

Possessives

Add **'s** to a person's name.

❸ Read

Read the ads and circle the occupations.

JOB ADS

1	2	3
4 Day Work Week ~~BUS DRIVER~~ Earn $14/hr Please call 916–555–0819 for an interview.	Immediate Openings for 3 Machinists Apply at: J&D Machine Co. 433 Ray Avenue Auburn, California 916–555–4321	SALESCLERK Experienced. Must work weekends. Food for Pets 11 Alvarado Street 916–555–7400
4	5	6
CASHIER WANTED Work 3 days a week. Apply in person: Shop and Go 873 Mission Street 916–555–1414	Smith Drugstore needs a Pharmacist for their Sacramento store. Call for an interview: 916–555–8700	DRIVER, Tow Truck. full time. Must live in Davis, experience necessary. 10 Johnson Road 916–555–0612

❹ Write

Write the occupations. Then write the street address or telephone number from each job ad.

	Occupation	Street Address	Telephone Number
Ad 1	Bus driver	-----	(916) 555-0819
Ad 2			
Ad 3			
Ad 4			
Ad 5			
Ad 6			

❶ Listening Review 🎧 019

Look at the pictures and listen. Choose the correct answer: *A*, *B*, or *C*.
Use the Answer Sheet.

1. A    B    C

Answer Sheet

1 (A) (B) (C)
2 (A) (B) (C)
3 (A) (B) (C)
4 (A) (B) (C)
5 (A) (B) (C)

2. A    B    C

3. A     B   C

4. A    B   C

5. A    B    C

❷ Dictation 🎧 020

Listen and write the sentences you hear.

1. _____ ?

2. _____ ?

3. _____ .

4. _____ .

5. _____ ?

❸ Grammar Review

Circle the correct answer: *A*, *B*, or *C*.

1. I _____ a student.
   A. am
   B. is
   C. are

2. He's from China. He _____ from Vietnam.
   A. 'm not
   B. isn't
   C. aren't

3. We _____ from Mexico.
   A. 'm
   B. 's
   C. 're

4. She _____ a student.
   A. 'm
   B. 's
   C. 're

5. She is from Haiti. _____ name is Marie.
   A. Your
   B. Her
   C. His

6. My name is Hector. What is _____ name?
   A. your
   B. my
   C. yours

LEARNING LOG

I know these words:

○ address
○ am
○ are
○ area code
○ ask
○ birthplace
○ board
○ book
○ bookbag
○ bus driver
○ cashier
○ chair
○ circle
○ city
○ clock

○ close
○ comma
○ computer
○ country
○ date of birth
○ dentist
○ desk
○ divorced
○ doctor
○ door
○ eight
○ eleven
○ eraser
○ female
○ fine

○ five
○ floor
○ four
○ fourteen
○ gender
○ go to
○ is
○ listen
○ machinist
○ male
○ map
○ marital status
○ married
○ middle name
○ Mr.

○ Mrs.
○ Ms.
○ nine
○ notebook
○ nurse
○ occupation
○ one
○ open
○ partner
○ pen
○ pencil
○ period
○ pharmacist
○ piece of paper
○ police officer

○ practice
○ question mark
○ raise
○ read
○ repeat
○ salesclerk
○ say
○ seven
○ single
○ sit down
○ six
○ stand up
○ state
○ street
○ student

○ table
○ take out
○ teacher
○ telephone number
○ ten
○ thirteen
○ three
○ twelve
○ two
○ wall
○ window
○ write
○ zero
○ zip code

I can ask:

○ What's your name?
○ Where are you from?
○ Where's the book?
○ What's on the wall?
○ How do you do?
○ What's Joan's occupation?

I can say:

○ I am from Mexico.
○ Nice to meet you.
○ It's on the table.
○ Open your book.
○ This is my friend, Gina.
○ Have a nice day.
○ She's a dentist.

I can write:

○ personal information
○ telephone numbers
○ zip codes
○ street addresses
○ numbers 0 to 14

Work-Out CD-ROM

Unit 1: Plug in and practice!

THINGS TO DO

❶ Learn New Words 021

Look at the pictures. Listen to the words. Then listen and repeat.

> There are classes, exercise rooms, concerts, and other activities at a community center.

❷ Listen and Write 022

Listen and write the telephone number next to each place.

1. hospital _____

2. drugstore _____

3. restaurant _____

4. laundromat _____

5. police station _____

6. supermarket _____

❸ Practice the Conversation 023

Look at the Eastville telephone book. Listen to the conversation. Then listen and repeat.

A: Where's the community center?

B: It's on Daniel Street.

A: What's the phone number?

B: It's 555-1547.

A: Thanks.

B: You're welcome.

G-18

E A S T V I L L E

EASTVILLE, CITY OF —
Community Center
    1135 Daniel Street.....................643-555-1547
Fire Station
    1170 High Street.......................643-555-1639
Library
    118 Low Street..........................643-555-4887
School, Adams
    154 State Street........................643-555-4600

Easy Moving Services
    Eastville Downtown office —
    80 Main Street..........................643-555-1300

Practice the conversation with a partner. Ask about the places in the Eastville telephone book.

Target Grammar

Simple present of *be*, *wh-* questions *page 150*

Public Services

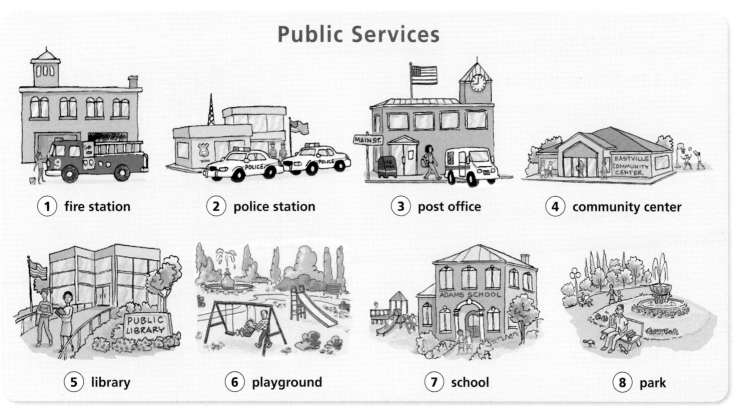

1. fire station
2. police station
3. post office
4. community center
5. library
6. playground
7. school
8. park

Businesses

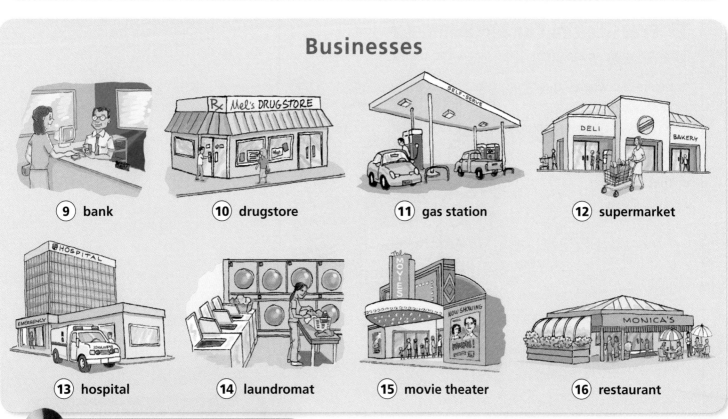

9. bank
10. drugstore
11. gas station
12. supermarket
13. hospital
14. laundromat
15. movie theater
16. restaurant

Work-Out CD-ROM

Unit 2: Plug in and practice!

Giving Directions

THINGS TO DO

❶ Learn New Words 024

Look at the pictures. Listen to the words. Then listen and repeat.

❷ Write

Work with a partner. Find the places in pictures 1 to 6 on the map on page 21. Write the places on the lines.

❸ Listen and Circle 025

Look at the map on page 21. Listen to the questions and circle *yes* or *no*.

1.	(Yes)	*No*	**4.**	*Yes*	*No*
2.	*Yes*	*No*	**5.**	*Yes*	*No*
3.	*Yes*	*No*	**6.**	*Yes*	*No*

❹ Talk about the Picture

Look at the map. Talk about the places.

Example: ***The bank is across from the post office.***

❺ Practice the Conversation 026

Listen to the conversation. Then listen and repeat.

A: Excuse me. Where's the post office ?

B: It's across from the bank .

A: Across from the bank ?

B: That's right.

A: Okay, thanks.

Practice the conversation with a partner. Ask about each place on the map.

① The post office is <u>next to</u> the drugstore.

④ The playground is <u>in front of</u> the school.

Target Grammar

Prepositions of place   *page 152*

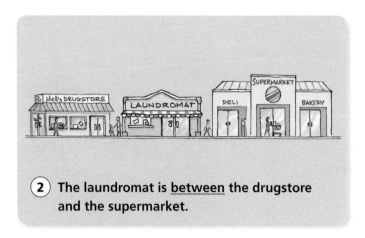

2 The laundromat is <u>between</u> the drugstore and the supermarket.

3 The bank is <u>across from</u> the post office.

5 There's a park <u>in back of</u> the library.

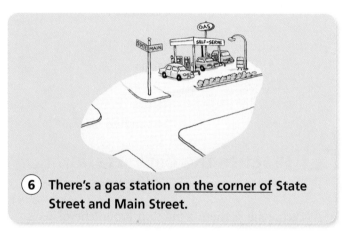

6 There's a gas station <u>on the corner of</u> State Street and Main Street.

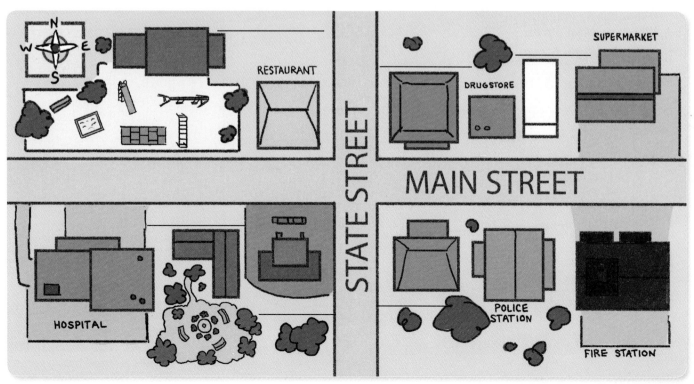

THINGS TO DO

❶ Talk about the Picture

Write 5 things about places in the picture. Share your ideas with the class.

Examples: *There's a post office on Pine Street.*
There's a restaurant next to the drugstore.

❷ Learn New Words 🎧 027

Look at the picture. Listen to the words. Then listen and repeat.

① parking lot
② crosswalk
③ bus stop
④ bus
⑤ ambulance
⑥ sidewalk
⑦ truck

⑧ stoplight
⑨ mailbox
⑩ ATM
⑪ pay phone
⑫ taxi
⑬ car
⑭ vending machine

⑮ stop
⑯ no parking
⑰ do not enter
⑱ no right turn
⑲ no left turn
⑳ one way

❸ Practice the Conversation 🎧 028

Listen to the conversation. Then listen and repeat.

A: Excuse me. Is there a bus stop around here?

B: Yes, there is. There's one on Main Street.

A. Where on Main Street?

B. In front of the movie theater .

A: Thanks a lot.

Practice the conversation with a partner. Ask about these things.

1	2	3

in front of / ?	next to / ?	in front of / ?

4	5	6

across from / ?	between / ?	next to / ?

Target Grammar

There is / there are   page 153

THINGS TO DO

❶ Talk about the Picture

Answer the questions.

Questions	Answers
a. What states are next to Florida?	Alabama and Georgia
b. What countries are next to the United States?	
c. What state is between Texas and Arizona?	

Write 3 questions about places in the U.S. Ask a partner your questions.

❷ Learn New Words 🎧 029

Look at the picture. Listen to the words. Then listen and repeat.

① capital   ② north   ③ south   ④ east   ⑤ west

Write the words on the lines below.

1. The _____ capital _____ of California is Sacramento.

2. New York is _____ of Pennsylvania.

3. Mexico is _____ of the United States.

4. Georgia is _____ of Alabama.

5. Iowa is _____ of Illinois.

❸ Read

Read and answer the questions.

1. This state is north of Alabama and south of Kentucky. The capital of this state is Nashville. What state is it?

_____

2. This state is east of Utah and west of Kansas. The capital of this state is Denver. What state is it?

_____

WRITING TIP
Remember to capitalize the first letter in the names of streets, cities, states, and countries.

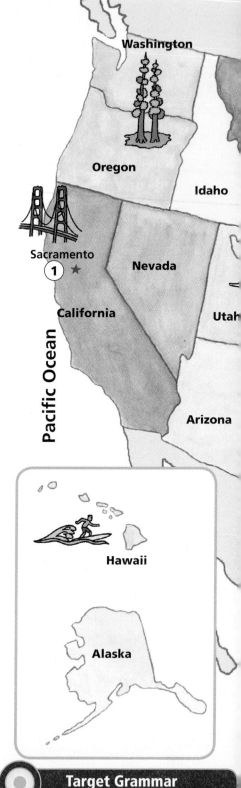

Target Grammar

Capitalization and punctuation *page 155*

Canada

2 N

5 W   E 4

3 S

Montana

North Dakota

Minnesota

New Hampshire   Maine

Vermont

Massachusetts

Wisconsin

South Dakota

Wyoming

Michigan

Lansing

Albany

New York

Rhode
Island

Connecticut

Nebraska

Iowa

Pennsylvania

Denver

Illinois   Indiana

Springfield

Ohio

Trenton

New Jersey

Colorado

Kansas

Missouri

Kentucky

Virginia

Delaware

Maryland

New Mexico

Oklahoma

Arkansas

Tennessee

Nashville

North Carolina

West Virginia

Atlanta

South Carolina

Mississippi

Georgia

Texas

Alabama

Louisiana

Tallahassee

Austin

Florida

Mexico

The state government is
in the state capital.

1 **Practice Pronunciation: Intonation** 030

> Intonation is when your voice goes up and down.

A. Listen to the sentences. Then listen and repeat.

Use "Excuse me?" when you don't understand.

1. A: Is there a restaurant around here?
B: Excuse me?

2. A: The post office is on Pine Street.
B: Excuse me? I don't understand.

Use "Excuse me." to get attention.

3. A: Excuse me. Is there a drugstore near here?
B: Yes, there is. There's one on Maple Street.

4. A: Excuse me. Where's the ATM?
B: There's one at the bank on the corner.

B. Listen to the sentences. Check the correct use of *Excuse me.* 031

	You don't understand	You want to get attention
1.	✔	
2.		
3.		
4.		
5.		

2 **Practice the Conversation: Asking for Repetition** 032

Listen to the conversation. Then listen and repeat.

A: Is there a restaurant near here?

B: Excuse me ?

A: Is there a restaurant near here?

B: Yes, there is. There's one on Pine Street .

A: Thanks.

Practice the conversation with a partner. Use these items.

1 a supermarket	**2** an ATM	**3** a bank	**4** a post office	**5** a park
I'm sorry, what was that?	Pardon?	What was that?	Could you repeat that?	Could you say that again?
Main Street	Maple Street	Maple Street	Pine Street	State Street

❸ Practice the Conversation: Saying You Don't Know 🎧 033

Listen to the conversation. Then listen and repeat.

A: Excuse me. Is there a drugstore near here?

B: I'm not sure .

A: Okay. Thanks anyway.

Practice the conversation with a partner. Use these items.

Sorry, I don't know.

Sorry, I'm new in town.

Sorry, I'm not sure.

Sorry, I don't know.

❹ Practice the Conversation: Saying You Don't Understand 🎧 034

Listen to the conversation. Then listen and repeat.

A: Is Pine Street north of Main Street?

B: I don't understand . I'm sorry.

A: That's okay. I'll ask someone else .

Practice the conversation with a partner. Use these items.

1 I don't know what you mean.

That's okay. I'll ask a police officer.

2 I don't speak English very well.

That's okay. Don't worry.

3 I don't understand.

No problem. Thanks anyway.

4 Excuse me?

Never mind. I can ask someone else.

❶ Learn New Words 🎧 035

Look at the pictures. Listen to the words. Then listen and repeat.

❷ Read

Read the questions and answers with a partner.

(1) librarian

(2) checkout desk

(3) library card

No. _____   Name _____

Edwards Public Library
42 Linsdale Ave.
Springfield, Illinois

Present this card each time you borrow a book.
You are responsible for books borrowed on this card.

How do I get a library card?
Go to the checkout desk and complete an application.
Show proof of your address. Your card is free.

(4) magazines

(5) audio CDs

(6) video DVDs

What can I take out from the library?
You can take out books, magazines, audio CDs, and DVDs.

7 children's books

What's in the library for children?
There are a lot of books for children.
There is also a story-telling program.

Are there any computers in the library?
Yes, there are. You can use the computers in the library.

❸ Write

Complete this library card application form.

🏛 Edwards Public Library

Application for an Adult Library Card

Part 1   Please print clearly. Enter only one letter or number per box.

[ ]
Last Name

[ ][ ][ ][ ][ ][ ][ ][ ][ ][ ][ ][ ][ ]   [ ][ ][ ][ ][ ][ ][ ][ ][ ][ ][ ][ ][ ]
First Name   Middle Name or Initial

[ ][ ][ ][ ][ ][ ][ ][ ][ ][ ][ ][ ][ ][ ][ ][ ][ ][ ]   [ ][ ][ ][ ]
Street Address   Apt.#

[ ][ ][ ][ ][ ][ ][ ][ ][ ][ ][ ][ ][ ][ ][ ]   [ ][ ]   [ ][ ][ ][ ][ ]
City   State   Zip Code

[ ][ ][ ]   [ ][ ][ ][ ][ ][ ]   _____
Area Code   Phone Number   Email address

Part 2 Please choose an easy-to-remember four-digit Personal Identification Number (PIN).

Numbers only, no letters. [ ][ ][ ][ ]

Part 3 Please read the statement and then sign your name.
I agree to be responsible for all materials borrowed against my Edwards Public Library card. I will notify the library immediately if my address changes or if my card is lost.

_____
Signature

What Do You Know?

① Listening Review 036

You will hear a question. Listen to the conversation. You will hear the question again. Choose the correct answer: *A*, *B*, or *C*. Use the Answer Sheet.

1. A. on Pine Street
   B. on Main Street
   C. on Front Street

2. A. next to the bank
   B. next to the restaurant
   C. next to the supermarket

3. A. on Pine Street
   B. on Green Street
   C. on Main Street

4. A. No, there isn't.
   B. Yes, there is.
   C. I don't know.

5. A. She doesn't know.
   B. She doesn't understand.
   C. She's new in town.

Answer Sheet

1 (A) (B) (C)
2 (A) (B) (C)
3 (A) (B) (C)
4 (A) (B) (C)
5 (A) (B) (C)

② Dictation 037

Listen and write the words you hear.

1. A: Excuse me. Where's _____?
   B: It's on Pine Street.

2. A: Excuse me. Is there _____ near here?
   B: Yes, there is. It's in front of the library.

3. A: What's _____ of New Mexico?
   B: I'm not sure.

4. A: Excuse me. Is there a _____?
   B: I'm sorry. I don't know.

5. A: What states _____ of Canada?
   B: I'm not sure.

❸ Grammar Review

Circle the correct answer: *A*, *B*, or *C*.

1. There _____ a drugstore on the corner.
   A. am
   B. is
   C. are

2. There _____ three parks in Eastville.
   A. am
   B. is
   C. are

3. _____ the fire station?
   A. Where are
   B. Where
   C. Where is

4. The school is next _____ the bank.
   A. to
   B. of
   C. on

5. The bus stop is _____ front of the ATM.
   A. of
   B. to
   C. in

6. _____ a parking lot on Main Street?
   A. Is there
   B. Are there
   C. There are

LEARNING LOG

I know these words:

- ○ across from
- ○ ambulance
- ○ ATM
- ○ audio CDs
- ○ bank
- ○ between
- ○ bus
- ○ bus stop
- ○ capital
- ○ car
- ○ checkout desk

- ○ community center
- ○ crosswalk
- ○ do not enter
- ○ drugstore
- ○ east
- ○ enter
- ○ fire station
- ○ gas station
- ○ hospital
- ○ in back of
- ○ in front of

- ○ laundromat
- ○ left
- ○ librarian
- ○ library
- ○ library card
- ○ magazine
- ○ mailbox
- ○ movie theater
- ○ near
- ○ next to
- ○ no left turn
- ○ no parking

- ○ no right turn
- ○ north
- ○ on the corner of
- ○ one way
- ○ park
- ○ parking lot
- ○ pay phone
- ○ playground
- ○ police station
- ○ post office
- ○ restaurant
- ○ right

- ○ school
- ○ sidewalk
- ○ south
- ○ stop
- ○ stoplight
- ○ supermarket
- ○ taxi
- ○ truck
- ○ turn
- ○ vending machine
- ○ video DVDs
- ○ west

I can ask:

- ○ Where's the post office?
- ○ Is there a restaurant near here?
- ○ Excuse me?

I can say:

- ○ The library is next to the police station.
- ○ There's a supermarket on Pine Street.
- ○ There are five banks near here.
- ○ I don't understand.
- ○ I'm not sure.

I can write:

- ○ an application for a library card

Work-Out CD-ROM

Unit 2: Plug in and Practice!

THINGS TO DO

❶ Learn Numbers 🎧 038

Listen to the numbers. Then listen and repeat.

11 eleven	12 twelve	13 thirteen	14 fourteen	15 fifteen
16 sixteen	17 seventeen	18 eighteen	19 nineteen	20 twenty
21 twenty-one	22 twenty-two	30 thirty	40 forty	50 fifty
60 sixty	70 seventy	80 eighty	90 ninety	100 one hundred

❷ Learn New Words 🎧 039

Look at the pictures. Listen to the words. Then listen and repeat.

❸ Practice the Conversation 🎧 040

Listen to the conversation. Then listen and repeat.

A: Excuse me. What time is it?

B: It's two o'clock.

A: Two o'clock?

B: That's right.

Practice the conversation with a partner. Use the clocks below.

 1
 **2**
 3
 **4**

 **5**
 **6**
 **7**
 **8**

❹ Listen and Write 🎧 041

Listen and write the times.

1. It's _____4:30_____.

2. It's _____.

3. It's _____.

4. It's _____.

5. It's _____.

6. It's _____.

1 1:00
It's one o'clock.

5 It's noon. (12:00 P.M.)

9 It's eight o'clock in the morning.

2 3:15
It's three-fifteen.
It's quarter after three.

3 5:30
It's five-thirty.

4 7:45
It's seven forty-five.
It's quarter to eight.

6 It's midnight. (12:00 A.M.)

7 It's 9:00 A.M.

8 It's 9:00 P.M.

10 It's two-fifteen in the afternoon.

11 It's seven-thirty in the evening.

12 It's eleven forty-five at night.

Work-Out CD-ROM
Unit 3: Plug in and Practice!

an analog clock = a clock with "hands" and numbers
a digital clock = a clock with numbers only

THINGS TO DO

❶ Learn New Words 🎧 042

Look at the picture. Listen to the words. Then listen and repeat.

① open
② closed
③ Sunday
④ Monday
⑤ Tuesday
⑥ Wednesday
⑦ Thursday
⑧ Friday
⑨ Saturday
⑩ No smoking
⑪ No eating
⑫ No cell phones

❷ Talk about the Picture

Write 5 things about the picture. Share your ideas with the class.

Example: *There are people in front of the library.*

❸ Practice the Conversation 🎧 043

Listen to the conversation. Then listen and repeat.

A: Is the library open on Saturday?

B: Yes, it's open from 10:00 to 5:30.

A: From 10:00 to 5:30?

B: Right.

Practice the conversation with a partner. Use the sign in the picture.

❹ Listen and Circle 🎧 044

Listen. Look at the picture. Circle the correct answer.

1. Yes, it is. / No, it isn't.
2. Yes, there are. / No, there aren't.
3. Yes, there are. / No, there aren't.
4. Yes, there is. / No, there isn't.
5. Yes, there is. / No, there isn't.
6. Yes, it is. / No, it isn't.

❺ Write

Write the hours of your library or school. Then share the hours with the class.

Example: *Sunday*   *9:00 A.M. to 5:00 P.M.*
          Monday   *9:00 A.M. to 7:00 P.M.*

Target Grammar

Simple Present of *be*, yes/no questions   *page 156*

THINGS TO DO

❶ Learn New Words 045

Look at the pictures. Listen to the words. Then listen and repeat.

❷ Write

Add the coins. Write the total on the line.

1. twenty-six cents (26¢)

2. _____

3. _____

4. _____

❸ Practice the Conversation 046

Listen to the conversation. Then listen and repeat.

A: How much is the table ?

B: It's $40.75.

A: Okay. Thank you.

Practice the conversation with a partner. Use these items.

1.

$2.25

2.

$14.50

3.

$365

4.

10¢

5.

$11.95

6.

$89

7.

$29.99

8.

$10.95

9.

$.75

Coins

① a penny (one cent/1¢)

② a nickel (five cents/5¢)

③ a dime (ten cents/10¢)

④ a quarter (twenty-five cents/25¢)

⑤ a one-dollar coin (one dollar/$1.00)

Target Grammar

Questions with *how much* and *how many*   page 158

Bills

6 **a one-dollar bill**
(a dollar/$1.00)

7 **a five-dollar bill**
(five dollars/$5.00)

8 **a ten-dollar bill**
(ten dollars/$10.00)

9 **a twenty-dollar bill**
(twenty dollars/$20.00)

10 **a fifty-dollar bill**
(fifty dollars/$50.00)

11 **a one hundred-dollar bill**
(one hundred dollars/$100.00)

12 (one thousand dollars/$1,000.00)

WINDOW ON MATH

Questions with *How much* 047

A Read the questions and answers.

Questions	Answers
<u>How much</u> is it?	It's fifty cents.
<u>How much</u> is the pen?	It's one dollar.
<u>How much</u> is a late book?	It's five cents a day.

B Work with a partner. Ask and answer 5 questions.

	a penny		a penny?
	a nickel		a nickel?
How much is	a dime	and	a dime?
	a quarter		a quarter?
	a dollar		a dollar?
	_____		_____?

Example: A: *How much is a penny and
a quarter?*
B: *It's twenty-six cents (26¢).*

Reading and Writing Checks

THINGS TO DO

❶ Learn New Words 🎧 048

Look at the checks. Listen to the words. Then listen and repeat.

① check ③ amount ⑤ memo
② check number ④ signature ⑥ account number

❷ Read and Write

Complete this chart with information from the 3 checks.

Check #	To	Amount	For (Memo)
124	Coral Beach Library	$12.75	late books
125			
126			

WRITING TIP

- Use a hyphen (-) for two-word numbers like "twenty-one."
- Use "and" between the dollar and cent amounts.

❸ Write

Write the check amounts.

1. $25.00   Twenty-five and 00/100 dollars
2. $31.50 _____
3. $56.34 _____
4. $108.29 _____

Then write a check to Ace Drugstore for $53.10.

```
┌─────────────────────────────────────────────────────┐
│  DAVID CAMPOS                              127        │
│    35 Hay St., Apt. 3C                                │
│  Coral Beach, FL 33915        DATE_____       │
│                                                       │
│  PAY TO THE                                           │
│  ORDER OF_____  $ [      ] │
│                                                       │
│  _____  DOLLARS      │
│                                                       │
│    TRUE BANK                                          │
│    Florida                                            │
│                                                       │
│  MEMO_____  _____         │
│  ⑈012345678⑈  123⑈456 7⑈ 0127                         │
└─────────────────────────────────────────────────────┘
```

Target Grammar

Capitalization with proper nouns   *page 160*

1 **DAVID CAMPOS** 124 2
35 Hay St., Apt. 3C
Coral Beach, FL 33915

DATE 8/19/12

PAY TO THE
ORDER OF Coral Beach Library $ 12.75 3

Twelve and 75/100 DOLLARS

TRUE BANK
Florida

MEMO for late books David Campos

⑆012345678⑉ 123⑈456 7⑈ 0124

DAVID CAMPOS
35 Hay St., Apt. 3C
Coral Beach, FL 33915

DATE 8/23/12 125

PAY TO THE
ORDER OF CASH

$ 50.00

Fifty and 00/100
TRUE BANK DOLLARS
Florida

MEMO for food 5 David Campos 4

⑆012345678⑉ 123⑈456 7⑈ 0125

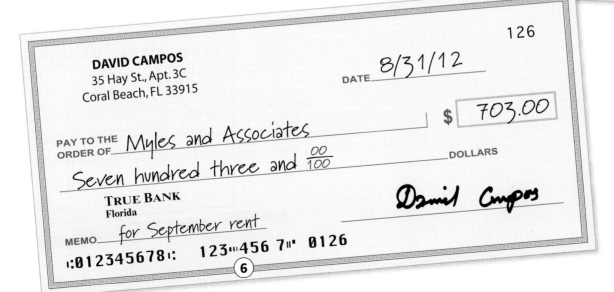

DAVID CAMPOS 126
35 Hay St., Apt. 3C
Coral Beach, FL 33915

DATE 8/31/12

$ 703.00

PAY TO THE
ORDER OF Myles and Associates

Seven hundred three and 00/100 DOLLARS

TRUE BANK David Campos
Florida

MEMO for September rent

⑆012345678⑉ 123⑈456 7⑈ 0126

6

LESSON 5

Making Phone Calls

1 **Practice Pronunciation: *Thirteen* or *Thirty*?** 049

A. Listen to the words. Then listen and repeat.

thirteen (13)	thirty (30)
fourteen (14)	forty (40)
fifteen (15)	fifty (50)
sixteen (16)	sixty (60)
seventeen (17)	seventy (70)
eighteen (18)	eighty (80)
nineteen (19)	ninety (90)

B. Listen and circle the numbers you hear.

1. 13   30   **3.** 15   50   **5.** 17   70   **7.** 19   90

2. 14   40   **4.** 16   60   **6.** 18   80

C. Listen and circle the numbers you hear.
   1. It's six-fifteen / six-fifty.
   2. It's fifteen cents / fifty cents.
   3. From 9:13 / 9:30 A.M. to 6:00 P.M.
   4. The price is $3.18 / $3.80.

Listen as your partner says the sentences. Repeat the numbers you hear.

2 **Practice the Conversation: Asking about Business Hours** 050

Listen to the conversation. Then listen and repeat.

A: Hello. Anderson's Drugstore. How can I help you?

B: Are you open on Thursday ?

A: Yes, we are.

B: What are your hours?

A: We're open from 8:00 to 6:00 .

B: Thank you.

Practice the conversation with a partner. Use the
information on the sign.

DRUG STORE HOURS
Sunday	noon–7:15
Monday	9:30–6:30
Tuesday	9:15–9:15
Wednesday	9:00–9:30
Thursday	8:00–6:00
Friday	8:30–6:30
Saturday	9:00–noon

❸ Practice the Conversation: Asking about Prices 051

Listen to the conversation. Then listen and repeat.

A: Horizon Bus Line. How may I help you?

B: Hi. How much is a ticket from Miami to Orlando ?

A: When are you traveling?

B: On October 6, in the morning .

A: There's a bus at 8:30 A.M. The fare is $45.50 .

Practice the conversation with a partner. Use these items.

1 Los Angeles to San Diego in the afternoon 3:15 P.M. $21.00	**2** Houston to Dallas in the evening 6:45 P.M. $43.50	**3** Santa Ana to San Francisco at noon 12:10 P.M. $54.00	**4** New York City to Rochester at night 9:17 P.M. $59.00	**5** Chicago to Springfield any time 8:13 P.M. $48.00

❹ Listen and Write: Listening to a Recorded Message 052

Listen and write the missing times. Then listen and check your answers.

Thank you for calling the Lucas Library.

For library hours, press 1.

The library is open Monday through Thursday from ___11:00___ to _____ .

On Friday and Saturday, the library is open from _____ to _____ .

It's closed on Sunday.

For information about our annual book sale, press 5.

Come to our book sale on March 30 from _____ to _____ .

There are great prices on used books.

Reading Paystubs

❶ Learn New Words 053

Listen to the story and read along. Find and circle these words in the story and on the paystub.

① pay rate   ② gross pay   ③ federal tax   ④ state tax   ⑤ net pay   ⑥ deductions

Bill is a salesclerk. He works in a supermarket. He works 40 hours a week. Bill's pay rate is $9.00 an hour. He earns $360.00 a week. This is his gross pay. He pays $23.30 to the U.S. government each week. This is his federal tax. He pays $11.14 to the California government. This is his state tax. His total deductions are $34.44. His net pay each week is $325.56. That is Bill's gross pay minus deductions.

Kim's Market
4426 Bay Street
Coral Beach, CA 95559

Employee: Bill Jackson
Social Security Number: 000-45-6789
Pay Period Date: 10/16/12 to 10/22/12

Check Number: **37288541**

EARNINGS	Pay Rate	Hours	This Period		Year-to-Date
	$9.00/hr	40	$360.00		$15,120.00
			$360.00	**GROSS PAY**	$15,120.00
DEDUCTIONS					
	Federal Tax		$ 23.30		$ 978.60
	State Tax		$ 11.14		$ 467.88
Total Deductions			$ 34.44		$1446.48
			$325.56	**NET PAY**	

❷ Write

Complete each sentence with a word from Activity 1.

1. Bill's _____ _____ is $9.00 an hour.

2. His _____ _____ is $360.00.

3. Bill's _____ _____ are $34.44.

4. His _____ _____ is $11.14.

5. His _____ _____ is $23.30.

6. His _____ _____ is $325.56.

❸ Read

Read the paystub. Answer the questions below.

Employee = Worker

Sonny's Diner   658 Red Rock Street, Coral Beach, CA 95559
Employee: Antonio Ruiz   Check Number: **19872**
Social Security Number: 000-40-2362
Pay Period Date: 5/5/12 to 5/11/12

EARNINGS	Pay Rate	Hours	This Period		Year-to-Date
	$12.00/hr	35	$420.00		$7,560.00
			$420.00	**GROSS PAY**	$7,560.00
DEDUCTIONS					
	Federal Tax		$ 63.00		$1,134.00
	State Tax		$ 37.80		$ 680.40
Total Deductions			$100.80		$1,814.40
			$319.20	**NET PAY**	

1. The employee's name is _____ *Antonio Ruiz* _____ .

2. The employee works at _____ .

3. This paystub is for the week of _____ to _____ .

4. This paystub is for _____ hours of work.

5. The employee's gross pay is _____ .

6. The employee's net pay is _____ .

❹ Listen and Write 054

Listen and fill in the missing information on the paystub.

May's Restaurant   556 Ocean Drive, Coral Beach, CA 95559
Employee: Stacy Ming   Check Number: **52871**
Social Security Number: 000-32-1598
Pay Period Date: 07/24/12 to 07/30/12

EARNINGS	Pay Rate	Hours	This Period		Year-to-Date
	$_____/hr	40	$406.00		$11,368.00
			$406.00	**GROSS PAY**	$11,368.00
DEDUCTIONS					
	Federal Tax		$_____		
	State Tax		$_____		
Total Deductions			$_____		
			$_____	**NET PAY**	

What Do You Know?

❶ Listening Review 055

Listen to the conversation. To finish the conversation, listen and choose the correct answer: *A*, *B*, or *C*. Use the Answer Sheet.

1. A. It's 9:00 A.M.
   B. We're open from 9:00 A.M. to 7:00 P.M.
   C. We close at 7:30 on Fridays.

2. A. It's $50.19.
   B. It's 9:15.
   C. We open at 9:00.

3. A. It's closed on Monday.
   B. It's $4.00.
   C. It's at 4:00.

4. A. It's $6.50.
   B. We're not open then.
   C. Yes, it is.

5. A. Okay. Here are three quarters.
   B. Okay. Here are two quarters.
   C. Yes, it is.

Answer Sheet

1 (A) (B) (C)
2 (A) (B) (C)
3 (A) (B) (C)
4 (A) (B) (C)
5 (A) (B) (C)

❷ Dictation 056

Listen and write the sentences you hear.

1. _____

2. _____

3. _____

4. _____

5. _____

Work-Out CD-ROM

Unit 3: Plug in and practice!

❸ Grammar Review

Circle the correct answer: *A, B,* or *C.*

1. How _____ coins are there?
- A. are
- B. much
- C. many

2. _____ the computer?
- A. How much
- B. How much are
- C. How much is

3. _____ the books $6.00?
- A. Are
- B. Is
- C. Be

4. She works on _____.
- A. baker street
- B. Baker Street
- C. Baker street

5. _____ the library open today?
- A. Are
- B. Is
- C. Be

6. He works at _____.
- A. Blue Horizon Restaurant
- B. Blue horizon restaurant
- C. blue horizon restaurant

LEARNING LOG

I know these words:

○ account number	○ closed	○ fifteen	○ morning	○ penny	○ Sunday
○ after	○ coin	○ fifty	○ net pay	○ P.M.	○ thirteen
○ afternoon	○ deductions	○ forty	○ nickel	○ quarter	○ thirty
○ A.M.	○ dime	○ fourteen	○ night	○ Saturday	○ Thursday
○ amount	○ dollar	○ Friday	○ nineteen	○ seventeen	○ Tuesday
○ bill	○ eating	○ gross pay	○ ninety	○ seventy	○ twelve
○ cell phone	○ eighteen	○ hours	○ noon	○ signature	○ twenty
○ cents	○ eighty	○ memo	○ o'clock	○ sixteen	○ twenty-one
○ check	○ eleven	○ midnight	○ one hundred	○ sixty	○ twenty-two
○ check number	○ evening	○ minute	○ open	○ smoking	○ Wednesday
	○ federal tax	○ Monday	○ pay rate	○ state tax	

I can ask:

- ○ What time is it?
- ○ Is the library open on Sunday?
- ○ What are your hours?
- ○ How much is it?

I can say:

- ○ It's two o'clock.
- ○ That's right.
- ○ It's open from noon to 9:00.
- ○ It's fifty cents.

I can write:

- ○ numbers 11 to 100
- ○ a personal check
- ○ amounts of money

THINGS TO DO

❶ Learn New Words 🎧 057
Look at the pictures. Listen to the words. Then listen and repeat.

❷ Ask Questions
Talk to 5 classmates. Write their answers in the chart.

Example: A: When is your birthday?
B: It's in September.

Name	Birthday
Mei	September

❸ Write
Complete the sentences. Then read your sentences to a partner.
1. This month is _____.
2. It's hot here in _____.
3. It's cold here in _____.
4. Next month is _____.
5. My favorite month is _____.

❹ Listen and Circle 🎧 058
Listen to the conversations. Circle the correct word.

1. June   July   January
2. March   April   May
3. October   November   December
4. cold   cloudy   cool
5. snowy   windy   sunny
6. rainy   cold   cloudy

1 January

7 July

13 hot

Months of the Year

2 February

3 March

4 April

5 May

6 June

8 August

9 September

10 October

11 November

12 December

Weather Words

14 warm

15 sunny

16 snowy

17 cold

18 cool

19 cloudy

20 rainy

21 windy

Work-Out CD-ROM

Unit 4: Plug in and practice!

Events on a Calendar

THINGS TO DO

❶ Learn Ordinal Numbers 059

Listen to the numbers. Then listen and repeat.

1st first	2nd second	3rd third	4th fourth
5th fifth	6th sixth	7th seventh	8th eighth
9th ninth	10th tenth	11th eleventh	12th twelfth
13th thirteenth	14th fourteenth	15th fifteenth	16th sixteenth

❷ Learn New Words 060

Look at the pictures. Listen to the words. Then listen and repeat.

1. doctor's appointment
2. haircut appointment
3. computer class
4. birthday party
5. PTA meeting
6. job interview
7. basketball game
8. dental appointment

❸ Listen and Circle 061

Listen to the conversations. Look at the pictures. Circle *True* or *False*.

1. True   False
2. True   False
3. True   False
4. True   False
5. True   False
6. True   False

❹ Practice the Conversation 062

Listen to the conversation. Then listen and repeat.

A: When is Alice's dental appointment?

B: On Tuesday.

A: What date is that?

B: I think it's the fifteenth.

Practice the conversation with a partner. Use the pictures.

Sunday	Monday

Target Grammar
Possessive nouns   *page 161*

13

MAY

Keeping Track of Appointments

THINGS TO DO

❶ Learn Ordinal Numbers 063

Listen to the numbers. Then listen and repeat.

17th seventeenth	18th eighteenth	19th nineteenth	20th twentieth
21st twenty-first	22nd twenty-second	23rd twenty-third	24th twenty-fourth
25th twenty-fifth	26th twenty-sixth	27th twenty-seventh	28th twenty-eighth
29th twenty-ninth	30th thirtieth	31st thirty-first	

❷ Write

Complete the chart. Use the appointment cards and calendar.

Name	Date	Day	Time
Jake	June 22	Friday	10:00 A.M.
Sue			
Nina			
Kate			
Sam			

❸ Practice the Conversation 064

Listen to the conversation. Then listen and repeat.

A: When is Jake's appointment?

B: It's on June twenty-second .

A: What day is that?

B: Friday .

A: What time?

B: At 10:00 A.M.

Practice the conversation with a partner. Ask about appointments for these people.

1 Kate's   **2** Sam's   **3** Paul's   **4** Sue's   **5** Lisa's

---

Sue Chen

has an appointment on

Ⓜ TU   W   TH   F

June 18   @   _4 p.m._

Please call to cancel.

Jake Kim

HAS AN APPOINTMENT ON

June 22   AT   _10 a.m._

Please call to canel.

 Randolph Optometry
Next appointment for:

Lisa Baker

Date: _June 20_   Time: _4 p.m._

Mon.   Tues.   (Wed.)
Thurs.   Fri.

 Target Grammar

Prepositions of time   *page 162*

Nina Chavez
has an appointment on
June 27 @ 12 p.m.
M   TU   (W)   TH   F
Please call to cancel.

Appointment Card

Kate Maxwell

June 28 @ 11 a.m.

Mon.   Tues.   Wed.   (Thurs.)   Fri.

Name: Paul Walters
Your next appointment is on:
June 19 at 9 a.m.
Mon.   _Tues._   Wed.   Thurs.   Fri.

JUNE

SUN	MON	TUE	WED	THU	FRI	SAT
					1	2
3	4	5	6	7	8	9
10	11	12	13	14	15	16
17	18	19	20	21	22	23
24	25	26	27	28	29	30

Name: Sam Piper

Your next appointment is on:

June 21 at 9 a.m.

Please call to cancel.

WINDOW ON MATH

Writing Dates 🎧 065

A Listen to the dates. Then listen and repeat.
1. 12/25/09 = December 25, 2009
2. 1/1/07 = January 1, 2007
3. 8/19/11 = August 19, 2011
4. 11/4/80 = November 4, 1980

B Write the dates another way.
1. 3/6/80 = _____   3. April 11, 1944 = _____
2. 5/19/08 = _____   4. February 17, 2012 = _____

C What's the date today? Write it 2 ways.

_____   _____

LESSON 4

Identifying Holidays

THINGS TO DO

❶ Learn New Words 066

Look at the pictures. Listen to the words. Then listen and repeat.

❷ Read and Write

Read about important days in the United States. Take notes in the chart. Share your answers with a partner.

Name of Holiday	When?
1. New Year's Day	January 1
2.	
3.	
4.	
5.	
6.	
7.	
8.	

WRITING TIP

Use capital letters for the names of important days.

Examples: New Year's Day, Valentine's Day, Election Day

❸ Write

Complete the sentences. Then read your sentences to the class.

My favorite holiday is _____.

It is in_____.

❹ Listen and Circle 067

Listen to the conversations. Then circle the correct answers.

1. July 4th   January 1st

2. in May   in March

3. the first Monday in September   September 1st

4. February 4th   February 14th

5. on a Monday   on a Tuesday

---

① New Year's Day

For people in the United States, New Year's Day is on January 1. That's the first day of the new year.

At midnight on New Year's Eve, people say "Happy New Year!" and kiss their friends and family.

④ Memorial Day

Memorial Day is on the last Monday in May. On this day, people remember the military service men and women who died in wars.

Target Grammar

Adjective + noun   *page 164*

(2) Martin Luther King, Jr. Day

Martin Luther King, Jr. Day is on the third Monday in January. Dr. King wanted everyone to have the same rights.

(3) Valentine's Day

Valentine's Day is on February 14. People give friends and family heart-shaped cards, flowers, and chocolate.

(5) Independence Day

In the United States, Independence Day is on the fourth of July. On this day, people watch colorful fireworks.

(6) Labor Day

Labor Day is on the first Monday in September. This holiday is for workers in the United States.

(7) Election Day

Election Day is on the first Tuesday after the first Monday in November. On this day, people vote.

(8) Thanksgiving

Thanksgiving is a big holiday in the United States. It's on the fourth Thursday in November. Many families eat a big dinner together on this day.

LESSON 5

Scheduling Appointments

1 Practice Pronunciation: Short *A* and Long *A* 068

A Listen to the words. Then listen and repeat.

1. male	**5.** make	**9.** map	**13.** raise	**17.** state
2. gas	**6.** magazine	**10.** back	**14.** after	**18.** day
3. date	**7.** basketball	**11.** May	**15.** table	**19.** April
4. that	**8.** cashier	**12.** rainy	**16.** okay	**20.** sale

Write the words in the correct place.

Sounds like *a* in map (short *A*)	Sounds like letter *A* (long *A*)
gas that	male date

B Work with a partner. Ask and answer the questions.

1. Is Texas a city or a state?

2. What date is today?

3. What month is after April?

4. What days of the week is your class?

5. Is Saturday before or after Friday?

2 Practice the Conversation: Making an Appointment 069

Listen to the conversation. Then listen and repeat.

A: Dr. Lambert's office.

B: Yes, this is Jim Brown . I'd like to make an appointment.

A: Okay. Our next opening is on April 6th at 11:00 .

B: That's great. I'll take it.

Practice the conversation with a partner. Use these items.

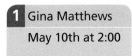

1 Gina Matthews
May 10th at 2:00

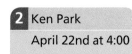

2 Ken Park
April 22nd at 4:00

3 Tom Lin
July 12th at 10:30

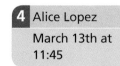

4 Alice Lopez
March 13th at 11:45

5 Margaret Song
May 3rd at 8:15

❸ Practice the Conversation: Canceling an Appointment 070

Listen to the conversation. Then listen and repeat.

A: Dr. Lambert's office.

B: This is Jim Brown . I need to cancel my appointment.

A: When is it?

B: It's on April 6th at 11:00 .

A: I'm sorry. April 5th ?

B: No, April 6th at 11:00 .

A: Okay. Thanks for calling.

Practice the conversation with a partner. Use these items.

1 Gina Matthews	2 Ken Park	3 Tom Lin	4 Alice Lopez	5 Margaret Song
May 10th at 2:00	April 22nd at 4:00	July 12th at 10:30	March 13th at 11:45	May 3rd at 8:15
May 9th?	3:00?	July 10th?	March 14th?	8:50?

❹ Practice the Conversation: Rescheduling an Appointment 071

Listen to the conversation. Then listen and repeat.

A: Dr. Lambert's office.

B: This is Jim Brown . I need to reschedule my appointment.

A: Okay. I have an opening on May 6th at 2:00 .

B: I'm sorry. I have a dental appointment at that time.

A: How about May 17th at 3:30 ?

B: That's good. Thank you.

Practice the conversation with a partner. Use these items.

1 Gina Matthews	2 Ken Park	3 Tom Lin	4 Alice Lopez	5 Margaret Song
May 12th at 5:00	May 16th at 3:00	July 28th at 4:15	March 20th at 8:00	May 10th at 2:10
haircut appointment	soccer game	PTA meeting	computer class	birthday party
May 13th at 2:15	May 17th at 1:30	August 1st at 8:00	March 23rd at 8:30	May 12th at 4:20

❶ Read

Read the school calendar. Answer the questions below.

SOUTH BEACH CITY PUBLIC SCHOOLS

First Semester

September 2 (Mon.)	Labor Day (Holiday – Schools Closed)
September 3 (Tues.)	First Day of School
October 4 (Fri.)	Class Pictures
November 11 (Mon.)	Veteran's Day (Holiday – Schools Closed)
November 12 (Tues.)	Progress Reports Issued
November 13 (Wed.)	Parent-Teacher Meetings
November 28 and 29 (Thurs., Fri.)	Thanksgiving (Holiday – Schools Closed)
December 11 (Wed.)	Report Cards Issued
December 23 – January 1	Winter Holidays (Schools Closed)

REPORT CARD

SOUTH BEACH CITY MIDDLE SCHOOL

Student Name: Brian Teese
Student ID: 7470

Grade: 07
Year: 2009-10

Course	Number	Teacher	Term 1	Term 2
English	112	Mearek, S	A	A
World Civics	211	Colman, D	B-	B+
Science	311	Bennet, H	B	B+
Math	421	Tambrey, J	A	A
Italian	722	Fabriano, C	C+	B-
Phys Ed	350	Langdon, J	A-	A

Absences: 3
Late: 0

1. When is the first day of school in South Beach?

_____

2. What holiday is in September?

_____

3. When are the schools closed in November?

_____

4. How many holidays are there between September 1 and December 1?

_____

5. When are report cards issued?

_____

6. When do you think school opens after the Winter Holidays?

_____

> Traditional school calendar = September – June
> Vacation = July and August
> Some U.S. public schools are year-round.

2 Mark the Calendar

Write the South Beach school events and holidays on the calendar for November.

NOVEMBER

SUN	MON	TUE	WED	THU	FRI	SAT
					1	2
3	4	5	6	7	8	9
10	11	12 Progress Reports issued	13	14	15	16
17	18	19	20	21	22	23
24	25	26	27	28	29	30

3 Complete the Chart

Read the sign. Then complete the chart.

SOUTH BEACH CITY PUBLIC SCHOOLS
NEW STUDENT REGISTRATION

Come to the School Office to register your child for school this fall!

Registration dates: August 1–August 20

Bring: 1. Your child's birth certificate
2. A driver's license or I.D. card with your address on it
3. Your child's health records

For more information, call 305-555-0481

Where is registration?	When is registration?	What do you need?	How can you find more information?

❶ Listening Review 🎧 072

Look at the pictures and listen. Choose the correct answer: *A*, *B*, or *C*.
Use the Answer Sheet.

1. A   B   C

2. A   B   C

3. A   B   C

4. A   B   C

5. A  B C

Answer Sheet

1 (A) (B) (C)
2 (A) (B) (C)
3 (A) (B) (C)
4 (A) (B) (C)
5 (A) (B) (C)

❷ Dictation 🎧 073

Listen and write the sentences you hear.

1. _____

2. _____

3. _____

4. _____

5. _____

③ Grammar Review

Circle the correct answer: *A*, *B*, or *C*.

1. When is _____ job interview?
   A. Ken
   B. Ken is
   C. Ken's

2. _____ birthday is on February 19th.
   A. Mark
   B. Mark's
   C. Mark is

3. My birthday is _____ May 20th.
   A. on
   B. at
   C. in

4. It's a _____.
   A. cold day
   B. day cold
   C. day is cold

5. My appointment is _____ 3:15.
   A. in
   B. at
   C. on

6. Labor Day is a _____.
   A. fun
   B. fun holiday
   C. holiday fun

LEARNING LOG

I know these words:

- ○ appointment
- ○ April
- ○ August
- ○ basketball game
- ○ birthday party
- ○ cancel
- ○ cloudy
- ○ cold
- ○ computer class
- ○ cool
- ○ December
- ○ dental appointment

- ○ doctor's appointment
- ○ eighteenth
- ○ eighth
- ○ eleventh
- ○ February
- ○ fifteenth
- ○ fifth
- ○ first
- ○ fourteenth
- ○ fourth
- ○ haircut appointment

- ○ hot
- ○ January
- ○ job interview
- ○ July
- ○ June
- ○ March
- ○ May
- ○ month
- ○ nineteenth
- ○ ninth
- ○ November

- ○ October
- ○ PTA meeting
- ○ rainy
- ○ reschedule
- ○ second
- ○ September
- ○ seventeenth
- ○ seventh
- ○ sixteenth
- ○ sixth
- ○ snowy

- ○ sunny
- ○ tenth
- ○ third
- ○ thirteenth
- ○ thirtieth
- ○ twelfth
- ○ twentieth
- ○ warm
- ○ weather
- ○ windy

I can ask:

- ○ How's the weather?
- ○ When is your birthday?
- ○ What day is that?
- ○ When is your appointment?
- ○ When is Labor Day?

I can say:

- ○ It's on May first.
- ○ I'd like to make an appointment.
- ○ I need to cancel an appointment.
- ○ I need to reschedule my appointment.

I can write:

- ○ dates in two ways
- ○ appointments on a calendar

Work-Out CD-ROM

Unit 4: Plug in and practice!

THINGS TO DO

1 Learn New Words 🎧 074

Look at the pictures. Listen to the words. Then listen and repeat.

2 Practice the Conversation 🎧 075

Listen to the conversation. Then listen and repeat.

A: What color is the `coat`?

B: It's `green`.

A: What color are the `pants`?

B: They're `black`.

Practice the conversation with a partner. Use the items in the pictures.

3 Write

List 5 clothing items your classmates are wearing for each color in the chart.

blue	white	yellow
Ann's sweater	Juan's shirt	Mei's jacket

4 Listen and Match 🎧 076

Listen and match the names and the pictures.

1. Sylvia ___   2. Tricia ___   3. Nick ___   4. Mark ___   5. Amanda ___

 a
 b
 c
 d
 e

5 Write

Write 3 sentences about your classmate's clothes.

Example: *Ken is wearing a blue shirt.*

Clothes for Men

(1) necktie

(2) undershirt

(3) briefs

Clothes for Men and Women

Clothes for Women

④ T-shirt

⑤ shirt

⑥ sweater

⑦ coat

⑧ jacket

⑨ hat

⑮ skirt

⑩ pants

⑪ shorts

⑫ socks

⑯ dress

⑬ shoes

⑭ boots

Colors

⑰ blue		㉑ brown	
⑱ yellow		㉒ green	
⑲ red		㉓ purple	
⑳ black		㉔ white	

 Target Grammar

Present continuous,
statements *page 165*

THINGS TO DO

❶ Learn New Words 🎧 077

Look at the picture. Listen to the words. Then listen and repeat.

PEOPLE
1. cashier
2. customer
3. fitting room attendant

PLACES
4. department store
5. customer service
6. exit
7. entrance
8. fitting room

ACTIONS
9. coming into (the store)
10. going into (the elevator)
11. sleeping
12. leaving
13. running
14. buying (sweaters)
15. talking
16. trying on (a sweater)
17. helping (a customer)

❷ Talk about the Picture

Work with a partner. Ask and answer questions about the people in the picture.

Example: A: What's <u>Jill</u> doing?
 B: She's buying sweaters.

❸ Practice the Conversation 🎧 078

Listen to the conversation. Then listen and repeat.

A: Can I help you?

B: Yes, I'm looking for children's sweaters.

A: They're on the second floor in children's clothes.

B: Thank you.

STORE DIRECTORY

Children's Clothes	2nd floor
Children's Shoes	3rd floor
Women's Clothes	1st floor
Women's Coats	4th floor
Women's Shoes	3rd floor
Men's Clothes	1st floor
Men's Coats	4th floor
Men's Shoes	2nd floor
Sleepwear	3rd floor

Practice the conversation with a partner. Ask about these items. Use the store directory.

1. dresses
2. neckties
3. women's boots
4. skirts
5. men's shirts
6. children's shoes

❹ Listen and Circle 🎧 079

Listen to the conversations. Look at the picture. Circle *True* or *False*.

1. True   False
2. True   False
3. True   False
4. True   False
5. True   False

STORE DIRECTORY

Children's Clothes 2. floor
Children's Shoes 3. floor
Women's Clothes 1. floor
Women's Shoes 3. floor
Men's Clothes 1. floor
Men's Coats

Ed and Don

Karen

SCARVES

Target Grammar

Present continuous, questions *page 167*

Sizes and Prices

THINGS TO DO

❶ Learn New Words 🎧 080

Look at the pictures. Listen to the words. Then listen and repeat.

❷ Talk about the Pictures

Ask and answer questions with a partner.

> What size is the <u>dress</u>?

> How much is <u>that coat</u>?

> It's a <u>medium</u>.

> It's <u>thirty dollars</u>.

❸ Practice the Conversation 🎧 081

Listen to the conversation. Then listen and repeat.

A: Excuse me. Do you work here?

B: Yes, I do. How can I help you?

A: Is this T-shirt on sale?

B: Yes. It's only five dollars .

A: Wow! Five dollars ! That's a good price.

Practice the conversation with a partner. Ask about these items.

1 sweater   **2** shirt   **3** coat   **4** jacket   **5** dress

❹ Write

Buy 4 things from Lane's Department Store. Write the store receipt.

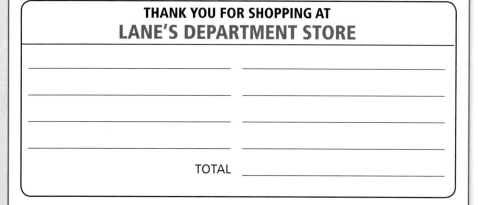

THANK YOU FOR SHOPPING AT
LANE'S DEPARTMENT STORE

_____ _____

_____ _____

_____ _____

_____ _____

TOTAL _____

SIZE: MEDIUM
$10.00
PRICE: $20.00

1 price tag

2 size

SIZE: SMALL
$25.00
PRICE: $50.00

SIZE: SMALL
$5.00
PRICE: $10.00

3 S (small)

Target Grammar

Demonstratives: *this, that, these, those*   *page 168*

4 M (medium)

SIZE: MEDIUM
$20.00
PRICE: $40.00

5 L (large)

SIZE: LARGE
$30.00
PRICE: $60.00

6 XL (extra large)

SIZE: EXTRA LARGE
$15.00
PRICE: $30.00

SALE

THANK YOU FOR SHOPPING AT

LANE'S DEPARTMENT STORE

T-shirt	$5.00
Shirt	$10.00
Coat	$30.00
Sweater	$15.00
Jacket	$25.00
Dress	$20.00
SUB-TOTAL	**$105.00**
8% TAX	**$8.40**
TOTAL	**$113.40**

7 receipt

WINDOW ON MATH

Multiplying

A Look at the examples.

One shirt costs $10.00. 1 x $10 = $10
Two shirts cost $20.00. 2 x $10 = $20
Three shirts cost $30.00. 3 x $10 = $30

B Complete the sentences.

1. One pair of pants costs $12. Three pairs of pants cost _____.

2. One sweater costs $15. Four sweaters cost _____.

3. One hat costs $11.50. Two hats cost _____.

4. One shirt costs $27. Four shirts cost _____.

5. One jacket costs $39. Five jackets cost _____.

6. One pair of shoes costs $35.25. Three pairs of shoes cost _____.

LESSON 4 — Identifying Clothes

THINGS TO DO

① Learn New Words 082

Look at the pictures. Listen to the words. Then listen and repeat.

① hole ② cutting ③ scissors ④ tailor

② Talk about the Pictures

Write a question about each picture. Then ask your classmates your questions.

Examples: *What is Leo wearing in picture one?*
What is Simon doing in picture one?

③ Listen and Read 083

Look at the pictures. Listen to the story. Then complete the story chart.

STORY CHART

At the beginning of the story, Leo is wearing _____.

Next, Leo is wearing _____.

Five years later, Leo is wearing _____.

④ Predict 084

What is the missing word at the end of the story? Share ideas with your classmates. Then listen and complete the sentence.

At the end of the story, Leo is wearing _____.

WRITING TIP

Use commas to separate three or more nouns in a sentence.
Use the word "and" before the final noun.
Example: *Leo is wearing blue pants, a red shirt, and a brown coat.*

⑤ Write

Write 2 sentences about what Leo or Simon is wearing in different pictures. In each sentence, list 3 things.

1. _____

_____

2. _____

_____

1

This is a story about Simon and Leo. Simon is a tailor. Leo is his friend. One day Leo comes into Simon's store. Leo is wearing a very old coat.

LEO: Oh, Simon, there is a big hole in my coat. What can I do?

3

Simon leaves the room with Leo's coat. After an hour, he comes back.

SIMON: Here you are, Leo. Your old coat is now a jacket.

LEO: Oh, Simon, it's beautiful. Thank you!

Target Grammar

Articles: *a, and an* *page 169*

2

Simon looks at the coat. Then he takes out his scissors.

LEO: What are you doing, Simon?

SIMON: I'm cutting your coat.

4

It is five years later.

LEO: Oh, Simon, there is a big hole in my jacket. What can I do?

Simon looks at the jacket. Then he leaves the room. After an hour, he comes back.

SIMON: Here you are, Leo. Your old jacket is now a vest.

LEO: Oh, Simon, it's beautiful. Thank you!

5

It is five years later.

LEO: Oh, Simon, there is a big hole in my vest. What can I do?

Simon looks at the vest. Then he leaves the room. After an hour, he comes back.

SIMON: Here you are, Leo. Your old vest is now a _____.

LEO: Oh, Simon, it's beautiful. Thank you!

Describing Clothes

❶ Practice Pronunciation: Vowel Sounds in *Shoes* and *Should* 085

> To say the vowel sound in *shoes*, make a circle with your mouth.
> To say the vowel sound in *should*, drop your jaw a little bit.

A. Listen to the words. Then listen and repeat.

1. shoes	should	loose	too
2. look	book	put	two
3. you	noon	woman	loose
4. took	you	good	could

Listen again. Circle the word that has a different vowel sound.

B. Listen to the words. Then listen and repeat. 086

1. blue   **a.** book

2. good   **b.** June

3. cook   **c.** shoe

4. noon   **d.** should

Work with a partner. Match the words that have the same vowel sound and the same ending sound.

❷ Learn New Words  087

Look at the pictures. Listen to the words. Then listen and repeat.

① long    ② too long    ③ short    ④ too short

⑤ tight    ⑥ too tight    ⑦ loose    ⑧ too loose

Describe the clothes in the pictures.

1. The red skirt isn't short. It's _____.

2. The purple skirt isn't too long. It's _____.

3. The brown pants aren't loose. They're _____.

4. The green pants aren't too tight. They're _____.

❸ Practice the Conversation: Describing Clothes 🎧 088

Listen to the conversation. Then listen and repeat.

A: What are you doing?

B: I'm trying on some clothes.

A: Let me see.

B: Okay. Do you like this dress ?

A: It's nice, but I think it's too short .

Practice the conversation with a partner. Use these items.

❹ Practice the Conversation: Returning Something 🎧 089

Listen to the conversation. Then listen and repeat.

A: I'd like to return these pants .

B: What's the problem?

A: They're too short .

B: All right .

Practice the conversation with a partner. Use these items.

1 shoes	2 shirt	3 dress	4 boots	5 briefs
tight	big	long	small	big
I'm sorry.	Okay.	Sure thing.	No problem.	All right.

6 jacket	7 pants	8 coat	9 shorts	10 sweater
short	loose	long	tight	big
That's no problem.	Sure. You can return them.	I'm sorry about that.	Okay.	No problem.

Work Clothes

❶ Write

What is each person wearing? Write a sentence about each person.

1. Ken    **2.** Lisa    **3.** Joe    **4.** Mei

1. _____

2. _____

3. _____

4. _____

❷ Give Opinions

Work with a partner. Match Ken, Lisa, Joe, and Mei to their occupations. Complete the sentences.

Occupations

dentist	bus driver	teacher	nurse	doctor
librarian	police officer	pharmacist	cashier	businessperson

A: What's Ken's occupation?

B: I think he's a _____.

A: Why is that?

B: Because he's wearing _____.

❸ Read and Write

Read the memo. Then complete the sentences about Leila, Phil, and Rob.

Smith Industries **MEMO**

To: All Employees **From:** Louis Smith
Topic: Work Clothes **Date:** August 1, 2012

All employees should dress appropriately. If your clothes are not appropriate, your supervisor may ask you to go home.

Inappropriate clothing includes the following:

• jeans

• shorts or short skirts

• baseball caps

• T-shirts

• sneakers

Leila

Leila's clothes are inappropriate for work because she is wearing

_____
_____
_____

Phil
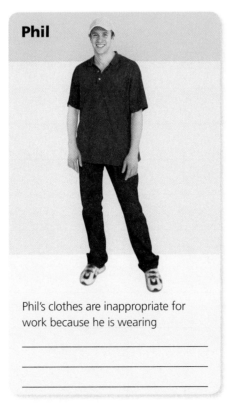
Phil's clothes are inappropriate for work because he is wearing

_____
_____
_____

Rob
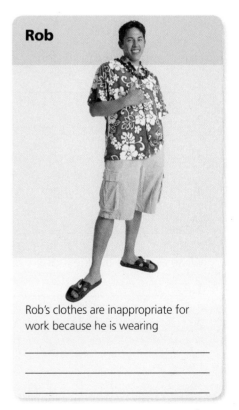
Rob's clothes are inappropriate for work because he is wearing

_____
_____
_____

What Do You Know?

① Listening Review 090

You will hear a question. Listen to the conversation. You will hear the question again. Choose the correct answer: *A*, *B*, or *C*. Use your Answer Sheet.

1. A. a blue sweater
   B. a blue shirt
   C. a blue necktie

2. A. She's buying a dress.
   B. She's trying on a dress.
   C. She's going into the fitting room.

3. A. $25.
   B. $20.
   C. On sale.

4. A. The dress is too long.
   B. The dress is too short.
   C. The dress is too loose.

5. A. a pair of pants
   B. a pair of shoes
   C. a tight jacket

Answer Sheet

1	Ⓐ	Ⓑ	Ⓒ
2	Ⓐ	Ⓑ	Ⓒ
3	Ⓐ	Ⓑ	Ⓒ
4	Ⓐ	Ⓑ	Ⓒ
5	Ⓐ	Ⓑ	Ⓒ

② Dictation 091

Listen and write the sentences you hear.

1. _____

2. _____

3. _____

4. _____

5. _____

Write answers to questions 1 and 2 above.

1. _____

2. _____

❸ Grammar Review

Circle the correct answer: *A*, *B*, or *C*.

1. Sue is wearing _____ dress today.
  A. a
  B. an
  C. of

2. What is _____?
  A. these
  B. that
  C. those

3. _____ you wearing a jacket?
  A. Are
  B. Is
  C. Be

4. Ted _____ into the store.
  A. are coming
  B. is come
  C. is coming

5. I'm buying _____ undershirt.
  A. a
  B. an
  C. two

6. _____ shoes are on sale.
  A. This
  B. That
  C. These

LEARNING LOG

I know these words:

- ○ baseball cap
- ○ black
- ○ blue
- ○ boots
- ○ briefs
- ○ brown
- ○ buying
- ○ cashier
- ○ coat
- ○ coming into
- ○ customer
- ○ customer service
- ○ cutting

- ○ department store
- ○ dress
- ○ entrance
- ○ exit
- ○ extra large
- ○ fitting room
- ○ fitting room
    attendant
- ○ going into
- ○ green
- ○ hat
- ○ helping
- ○ hole

- ○ jacket
- ○ jeans
- ○ large
- ○ leaving
- ○ long
- ○ loose
- ○ medium
- ○ necktie
- ○ pants
- ○ price tag
- ○ purple
- ○ receipt
- ○ red

- ○ running
- ○ scissors
- ○ shirt
- ○ shoes
- ○ short
- ○ shorts
- ○ size
- ○ skirt
- ○ sleeping
- ○ small
- ○ sneakers
- ○ socks
- ○ sweater

- ○ tailor
- ○ talking
- ○ tight
- ○ too
- ○ trying on
- ○ T-shirt
- ○ undershirt
- ○ wearing
- ○ white
- ○ yellow

I can ask:

- ○ What color is the jacket?
- ○ What's he doing?
- ○ What size is this shirt?
- ○ Do you like this dress?
- ○ Is this shirt on sale?
- ○ How much is that coat?

I can say:

- ○ I'm looking for children's clothes.
- ○ He's wearing a coat.
- ○ It's too short.
- ○ I'd like to return these pants.

I can write:

- ○ a store receipt
- ○ a sentence with three or more items

Work-Out CD-ROM

Unit 5: Plug in and practice!

UNIT 6 FOOD

LESSON 1 Identifying Foods

THINGS TO DO

❶ Learn New Words 092

Look at the pictures. Listen to the words. Then listen and repeat. Add another food to each group.

❷ Talk about the Picture

Work with a partner. Talk about the food in the pictures.

Example: *I like noodles.*   *I don't like cheese.*

❸ Listen and Check 093

Listen. Check the foods you hear.

○ apples	○ tomatoes	○ cheese	○ milk
○ carrots	○ lettuce	○ yogurt	○ ice cream
○ bread	○ cereal	○ beans	○ chicken
○ noodles	○ rice	○ fish	○ peanuts

❹ Practice the Conversation 094

Listen to the conversation. Then listen and repeat.

A: Do you go to the farmers' market every week?

B: Yes, I do. I usually go on Thursday .

A: We go there, too. I buy cheese and fruit .

B: The food is very good there.

Practice with a partner. Use the ideas below.

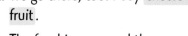

1 Friday	**2** Sunday	**3** Wednesday
tomatoes and apples	fruits and vegetables	lettuce and carrots

People sell fresh fruits and vegetables at a farmers' market.

Target Grammar

Simple present, statements *page 170*

Grains

 ① noodles

 ② bread

 ③ rice

 ④ cereal

_____

Meat, Fish, Beans, Nuts

 ⑬ peanuts

 ⑭ chicken

 ⑮ fish

 ⑯ beans

_____

Fruits

 5 apples

 6 oranges

 7 grapes

 **8** bananas

Dairy

 9 milk

 10 cheese

 11 yogurt

 12 ice cream

Food Groups

Vegetables

 17 onions

 18 tomatoes

 19 lettuce

 20 carrots

Fats, Oils, and Sweets

 **21** butter

 **22** oil

 23 sugar

Work-Out CD-ROM

Unit 6: Plug in and practice!

THINGS TO DO

❶ Learn New Words 🎧 095

Look at the pictures. Listen to the words. Then listen and repeat.

① aisle
② meat counter
③ checkout counter
④ bakery
⑤ produce section
⑥ manager
⑦ bag
⑧ cart
⑨ basket
⑩ coupons
⑪ push a cart
⑫ look at
⑬ eat
⑭ check out
⑮ stand in line

❷ Talk about the Picture

Write 5 things about the picture.

Examples: *Marcus is looking at coupons.*
Tina is standing in line.

Share your ideas with the class.

❸ Practice the Conversation 🎧 096

Listen to the conversation. Then listen and repeat.

A: Excuse me. Where's the rice ?

B: It's in Aisle 1 .

A: Thanks. And where are
the bananas ?

B: They're in the produce section .

A: Thank you.

B: You're welcome.

Practice the conversations with a partner. Ask about these items.
Add your own ideas.

Target Grammar

Count and noncount
nouns *page 172*

Using Quantity Words for Food

THINGS TO DO

❶ Learn New Words 097

Look at the picture. Listen to the words. Then listen and repeat.

- ① a bag of apples
- ② a head of lettuce
- ③ a carton of milk
- ④ a loaf of bread
- ⑤ a package of cheese
- ⑥ a jar of honey
- ⑦ a box of sugar
- ⑧ a pound of chicken
- ⑨ a can of tomatoes
- ⑩ a bottle of oil
- ⑪ expensive
- ⑫ cheap

What other foods are in the picture? Share your ideas with the class.

❷ Find Someone Who

Make a chart like this. Write 8 foods from the picture.

FOOD	PERSON'S NAME
1. a loaf of bread	Keiko
2. a jar of honey	Tina

Talk to your classmates. Find someone who has the food at home. Write the person's name.

Example: A: Do you have a loaf of bread at home?
B: Yes, I do. / No, I don't.

❸ Practice the Conversation 098

Listen to the conversation. Then listen and repeat.

A: Can I help you?

B: Yes. I need a loaf of bread . How much is it?

A: Five dollars.

B: Really? That's expensive!

Practice the conversation with a partner. Use these items.

Target Grammar

Want and *need*   *page 173*

THINGS TO DO

❶ Look at the Pictures

Look at the store flyers. Check the foods you see.

○ chicken   ○ cheese   ○ milk   ○ tomatoes   ○ orange juice

○ carrots   ○ oil   ○ onions   ○ green beans   ○ bread

❷ Read and Write

Read the store flyers for Ray's Supermarket and Ford's Supermarket. Write the price and amount of each food.

> 16 ounces (oz.) = one (1) pound (lb.)
> but 16 fluid ounces = one (1) quart

Food	Ray's Supermarket		Ford's Supermarket	
	Price	Amount	Price	Amount
green beans	$1.25	1 lb.		
chicken				
orange juice	$2.00	32 oz.		
vegetable oil				
carrots				

❸ Listen and Circle 099

Listen to the conversations and circle your answers.

1. a. at Ray's   b. at Ford's

2. a. $1.20 a pound   b. $.99 a pound

3. a. 96 ounces   b. 16 ounces

4. a. 10 pounds   b. 7 pounds

5. a. $3.99   b. $2.99

WRITING TIP

Use *and* to add information.
- Example: I need green beans and carrots.

❹ Write

Write 2 sentences about things you need. Use **and**. Read your sentences to a partner.

Example: ***What do you need at the store?***
             I need two boxes of cereal and a carton of milk.

Target Grammar

Simple present,
Wh- questions   *page 174*

FORD'S SUPERMARKET

 **2**⁹⁹ 16 oz. bottle

 **1**⁹⁹ 64 oz. carton

 **99**¢ a pound

Vegetable Oil

Orange Juice

Chicken Legs

 **99**¢ per pound

 **79**¢ per pound

Fresh Green Beans

Carrots

Prices That Can't Be Beat!

Ray's SUPERMARKET

THE SUPER SAVER!

 **2** FOR **$6**
• Carrots
5 lb. bag

 **1**²⁵ per pound
• Fresh Green Beans

32 oz. carton
• Orange Juice

96 oz. bottle
• Vegetable Oil

• Chicken Legs

2 FOR **$4**

3⁹⁹

1²⁰ per pound

LESSON 5 — Asking for Store Information

❶ Practice Pronunciation: Intonation in *Yes/No* Questions 100

When we ask *yes/no* questions, our voices go up at the end. We sometimes ask for a *yes* or *no* answer with only part of the question. *Anything else?* is an example.

A. Listen to the questions. Then listen and repeat.

1. Can I help you?
2. Do you have grape juice?
3. Is rice on sale this week?
4. Anything else?

5. Do you like noodles?
6. Do you have a package of cheese at home?
7. Are there apples in the produce section?
8. Are you standing in line?

Work with a partner. Ask and answer the questions.

B. Listen to the sentences. Then listen and repeat. 101

1. a. The apples are on sale ____
   b. The apples are on sale ____

2. a. Okay ____
   b. Okay ____

3. a. Milk ____
   b. Milk ____

4. a. Aisle 3 ____
   b. Aisle 3 ____

5. a. Anything else ____
   b. Nothing else ____

6. a. The produce section ____
   b. The produce section ____

Listen again. Write a period after each statement and a question mark after each question.

❷ Practice the Conversation: Asking for Help 102

Listen to the conversation. Then listen and repeat.

A: Can I help you?
B: Yes. Do you have vegetable oil ?
A: Yes, we do. It's on sale this week.
B: How much is it ?
A: It's $1.99 for a 64-ounce bottle.

Practice the conversation with a partner. Use these items.

1 cheese	2 rice	3 bread	4 sugar
$2.25 for a 10-ounce package	99¢ for a 16-oz. bag	$2.50 for a 24-oz. loaf	$3 a bag

5 carrots	6 apples	7 onions	8 oranges
$2 per pound	$3 for 5 pounds	$1.50 a pound	$4 a bag

❸ Practice the Conversation: Ordering Food at a Counter 103

Listen to the conversation. Then listen and repeat.

A: Number 27, please.

B: That's me.

A: What would you like?

B: Three pounds of cheese .

A: Three pounds?

B: Yes, please.

A: Anything else?

B: No, that's all.

Practice the conversation with a partner. Use these items.

1 half a pound of fish

2 two loaves of bread

3 three pounds of chicken

4 two pounds of cheese

5 five pounds of yogurt

6 twelve ounces of butter

7 half a pound of chicken salad

❹ Practice the Conversation: Asking about Sales  104

Listen to the conversation. Then listen and repeat.

A: Is milk on sale this week?

B: Yes. It's only 99 cents a carton .

A: What size?

B: 32 ounces .

A: Great! That's a really good price.

Practice the conversation with a partner. Use these items.

1 rice
$1 a bag
16 ounces

2 honey
$4 a jar
32 ounces

3 sugar
$1.25 a box
16 ounces

4 oil
$.99 a bottle
8 ounces

5 yogurt
$1.15 a bottle
12 ounces

6 orange juice
$3 a carton
64 ounces

7 cheese
$1.99 a package
8 ounces

8 cereal
$2.99 a box
15 ounces

Ordering from a Menu

❶ Learn New Words 105

Look at the menu. Listen to the words. Then listen and repeat.

Main Street Diner

Appetizers

Chicken soup	$3.95
Green salad	$4.50
Onion rings	$5.95
Fruit salad	$4.50

Main Courses

Hamburger	$6.95
Fish sandwich	$7.95
Pizza slice	$2.50
½ Chicken	$8.95

Side Dishes

Baked potato	$2.95
Green beans	$2.00
Corn	$2.00
Macaroni and cheese	$2.50

Beverages

Coffee	$1.50
Tea	$1.00
Milk	$2.00
Soda	$1.50

For a platter, main dish with one side dish and beverage, add $2.00.

1932 Main Street   Centerville   555-9200

❷ Listen and Write 106

Listen to the orders. Write what you hear.

Customer 1

Guest Check

TABLE NO.	NO. PERSONS	CHECK NO. 801922	SERVER NO.

Order		Price
Hamburger		
Milk		
	Subtotal	
	TAX	
	Total	

Thank You!

Customer 2

Guest Check

TABLE NO.	NO. PERSONS	CHECK NO. 801923	SERVER NO.

Order		Price
Green Beans		
	Subtotal	
	Tax	
	Total	

Thank You!

Read the menu. Write the prices for each order.

❸ Write

Answer the questions.

1. What is the subtotal bill for Customer 1? _____

2. What is the subtotal bill for Customer 2? _____

3. Which customer is having a platter? _____

4. Which customer is paying more?_____

❹ Practice the Conversation 107

Listen to the conversation. Then listen and repeat.

A: What would you like today?

B: I'd like a fish sandwich and a salad , please.

A: A fish sandwich and a salad . Anything to drink?

B: Yes. I'll have a cup of coffee , please.

Practice the conversation with a partner. Order new items from the menu.

Guest Check

TABLE NO.	NO. PERSONS	CHECK NO. 801924	SERVER NO.

TAX

Thank You!

WINDOW ON MATH

Calculating Tax

In many states, you have to add tax to a food bill. Tax is a percentage of the bill.

Example: *Subtotal is $15.00 and sales tax is 5%*
$15 × .05 = $.75
$15.00 + $.75 = $15.75

1. Calculate a 5% tax for Customer 1 from page 84.

Subtotal _____

Add 5% tax + _____

Total = _____

2. Calculate a 5% tax for Customer 2 from page 84.

Subtotal _____

Add 5% tax + _____

Total = _____

What Do You Know?

① Listening Review 108

Look at the pictures and listen. Choose the correct answer: *A*, *B*, or *C*. Use the Answer Sheet.

1. A 　　　B 　　　C

2. A 　　　B 　　　C

3. A　　　B　　　C

4. A 　　　B　　　C

5. A　　　B　　　C

Answer Sheet

1 (A)　(B)　(C)
2 (A)　(B)　(C)
3 (A)　(B)　(C)
4 (A)　(B)　(C)
5 (A)　(B)　(C)

② Dictation 109

Listen and write the sentences you hear.

1. _____

2. _____

3. _____

4. _____

5. _____

❸ Grammar Review

Circle the correct answer: *A*, *B*, or *C*.

1. Where_____ you live?

  A. are
  B. do
  C. does

2. We _____ a carton of milk.

  A. need
  B. needs
  C. needing

3. I drink a cup of _____ in the morning.

  A. coffee and milk
  B. coffees and milk
  C. coffee and milks

4. They _____ onions.

  A. doesn't like
  B. don't like
  C. don't likes

5. I ____ food at the supermarket.

  A. buy
  B. buys
  C. buying

6. What _____ she need?

  A. do
  B. does
  C. is

LEARNING LOG

I know these words:

- aisle
- anything
- appetizers
- apple
- bag
- baked potato
- bakery
- banana
- basket
- bean
- beverages
- bottle
- box
- bread
- butter
- can
- carrot

- cart
- carton
- cereal
- cheap
- check out
- checkout counter
- cheese
- chicken
- coffee
- corn
- coupons
- cup
- dairy
- eat
- expensive
- farmers' market
- fish

- food
- fruit
- grain
- grape
- hamburger
- head
- honey
- ice
- ice cream
- jar
- juice
- lettuce
- like
- loaf
- look at
- macaroni and cheese

- main courses
- manager
- meat
- menu
- milk
- noodles
- nut
- oil
- onion
- onion rings
- on sale
- orange
- ounce
- package
- peanut
- pizza

- pound
- produce section
- push a cart
- rice
- salad
- sandwich
- side dishes
- slice
- soda
- soup
- stand in line
- sugar
- tea
- tomato
- vegetable
- yogurt

I can ask:

- Do you go to the farmers' market?
- Where's the rice?
- How much is a loaf of bread?
- Is milk on sale?

I can say:

- Yes, I do.
- No, I don't.
- It's 99¢.
- A pound of chicken, please.
- It's in Aisle 3.
- I like noodles.
- I don't like cheese.

I can write:

- food words
- the price of foods
- a shopping list
- a food order

Work-Out CD-ROM

Unit 6: Plug in and practice!

UNIT 7 FAMILIES

THINGS TO DO

❶ Learn New Words 🎧 110

Look at the pictures of this family. Listen to the words. Then listen and repeat.

Make a chart like this. Write the family words.

Male	Female	Male or Female
husband	wife	parents

❷ Write

Write words on the lines to complete the sentences.

Jack and Mei have two _____. Jack and Mei have one _____ and one _____. Ann has one _____. She doesn't have a _____. Jack has one _____. He doesn't have a _____.

Write sentences about your family.

Example: *I have two sisters. I don't have cousins.*

❸ Listen and Match 🎧 111

Listen to the interview. Match the names to the relatives.

Relative	Name
1. husband __c__	a. Linda
2. son _____	b. Hannah
3. daughter _____	c. Mark
4. sister _____	d. Brad
5. niece _____	e. Karen

❹ Ask Questions

Work with a partner. Ask about your partner's family.

1. What is your mother's name? _____
2. What is your grandmother's name? _____
3. What is your husband's or wife's name? _____
4. Do you have a brother? What is your brother's name? _____
5. Your idea: _____

Jack   Mei

① husband   ② wife

Ann   Tim

⑨ sister   ⑩ brother

Target Grammar
Simple present of *have*   page 175

(3) parents (4) children

(5) daughter (6) mother

(7) son (8) father

(11) grandmother (12) grandson

(13) grandfather (14) granddaughter

(15) uncle (16) nephew

(17) aunt (18) niece

(19) cousins

Work-Out CD-ROM
Unit 7: Plug in and practice!

Family Responsibilities

THINGS TO DO

❶ Learn New Words 112

Look at the pictures. Listen to the words. Then listen and repeat

❷ Listen and Match 113

Listen to the conversation. Match the name to the responsibility.

1. Mei __b__   **a.** takes out the trash

2. Jack _____   **b.** cooks dinner

3. Ann _____   **c.** goes grocery shopping

4. Tim _____   **d.** does the laundry

5. Everyone in Mei's family _____   **e.** makes the bed

(1) **fix things**

❸ Interview

Work with a partner. Ask the questions below. Check (✔) your partner's answers.

Do You _____ ?	Yes	No
fix things at home	○	○
make the beds	○	○
wash the dishes	○	○
take out the trash	○	○
go grocery shopping	○	○
pay the bills	○	○
clean the house	○	○
do the laundry	○	○
cook dinner	○	○
feed the pets	○	○

(4) **take out the trash**

Share 3 things about your partner with the class.

Example: *My partner does the laundry.*

❹ Write

What do you do at home? What don't you do at home? Write sentences.

Example: *I cook dinner and clean the house.*
I wash the dishes and take out
the trash. I don't pay the bills.

(6) **pay the bills**

Target Grammar

Simple present,
Yes/No questions   *page 176*

(2) make the bed

(3) wash the dishes

Family Responsibilities

(5) go grocery shopping

(7) clean the house

(8) do the laundry

(9) cook dinner

(10) feed the pets

Recreation: At the Park

THINGS TO DO

❶ Learn New Words 114

Look at the picture. Listen to the words. Then listen and repeat.

Activities

① read the newspaper	⑥ listen to music
② play an instrument	⑦ play soccer
③ dance	⑧ tell stories
④ play cards	⑨ ride a bicycle
⑤ take pictures	⑩ have picnics

Feelings

⑪ happy
⑫ sad
⑬ angry
⑭ afraid
⑮ confused

❷ Talk about the Picture

Write 5 things about the picture. Then share your ideas with the class.

Example: *The man with the cap is playing an instrument.*
The boy with the yellow and blue shirt is happy.

❸ Interview

Ask your partner the questions below. Check (✔) your partner's answers.

Do the People in Your Family ____ ?	Yes, Often.	Yes, Sometimes.	No, Never.
listen to music	○	○	○
play cards	○	○	○
play instruments	○	○	○
tell stories	○	○	○
play soccer	○	○	○
dance	○	○	○

Share 3 things about your partner with the class.

Example: *Alyta's brother often plays cards.*

❹ Practice the Conversation 115

Listen to the conversation. Then listen and repeat.

A: What do you do on weekends?

B: I usually play soccer . What about you?

A: I listen to music .

B: That's nice.

Practice the conversation with a partner. Use the activities you like.

Target Grammar
Adverbs of frequency *page 178*

Family Portraits

THINGS TO DO

1 Before You Read

Look at the photos. Write the number of the photo next to the correct people.

husband and wife _____   aunt, uncle, niece _____

parents and daughters _____   mother and two sons _____

grandparents, children, and grandchildren _____

2 Read and Take Notes 116

Listen and read about each family. Take notes in the chart below.

Name	Marital Status	Lives with
1. Pilar	married	husband and 2 children
2. Boris		
3. Sonya		
4. Nhu Trinh		
5. Soraya		

Work with a partner. Tell about each person's family.

Example: *Pilar is married. She lives with her husband and her two children.*

3 Write

Write about people in your family.

1. I live with _____.

We live in _____.

2. My aunt's name is _____.

She is my _____ sister.

3. My uncle's name is _____.

He is my _____ brother.

4. My cousins' names are _____.

They are _____ children.

My name is Pilar Garcia and I'm from Mexico. I am married and I have two children. My husband's name is Manuel. My two daughters' names are Belen and Maria. We live together in Phoenix, and we are very happy.

My name is Sonya and I'm from China. I'm single. I live with my aunt and uncle. My uncle is my mother's brother. My mother and father live in China. I miss them very much.

Target Grammar

Compound sentences with
and and *but*   *page 180*

2

My name is Boris and I'm from Russia. My wife's name is Anna. We have many children and grandchildren. Now we live in a beautiful home with our daughter. My family is my whole life. I love my family.

4

My name is Nhu Trinh. I'm from Vietnam. I have three children. My husband and I live in California. I work at a bank in Los Angeles. My daughter and son-in-law live in Vietnam. My sons live in Arizona. I love my family, but we don't see each other very much.

5

My name is Soraya. I'm from Somalia. My husband's name is Karim. We have two sons now. We want more children. But first we need a bigger home! We want to buy a house. My husband and I work very hard.

LESSON 5 — Using the Telephone

❶ Practice Pronunciation: Linking Consonant to Vowel 117

> When one word ends with a consonant sound and the next word starts with a vowel sound, we say the two words together.

A. Listen to the words. Then listen and repeat.

1. is Ann	**4.** number is	**7.** take a
2. call Ed	**5.** can I	**8.** just a
3. this is	**6.** name is	**9.** did I

B. Listen to the sentences. Then listen and repeat. 118

1. Can I speak to Mike Elliot, please?

2. Can you ask him to call Ed Adams?

3. My number is 555-1234.

4. Just a minute.

5. His name is Bob Underwood.

Work with a partner. Circle the linking words in the sentences above.

❷ Practice the Conversation: Answering the Phone 119

Listen to the conversation. Then listen and repeat.

A: Hello.

B: Hi. Is Ann there?

A: Who is calling, please?

B: This is Pat. I'm her classmate.

A: Just a minute, please. I'll get her.

Practice the conversation with a partner. Use these items.

1 May I ask who's calling?
Sue / I play soccer with her.

2 May I have your name?
Dan / I'm her brother.

3 Can you tell me your name, please?
Maria / I play cards with her.

4 Who is calling, please?
Dr. Smith / I'm her dentist.

5 Who may I say is calling?
Ron Martin / I'm her uncle.

❸ Practice the Conversation: Taking a Message 120

Listen to the conversation. Then listen and repeat.

A: Can I speak to your father, please?

B: He's not here now. Can I take a message?

A: Can you ask him to call Mr. Rogers ? My number is 555–3598 .

B: Call Mr. Rogers at 555–3598 ?

A: Right. Thank you.

B: You're welcome. Good-bye.

Practice the conversation with a partner. Use these items.

1 Jeff	**2** Dr. Smith	**3** Ms. Tanaka	**4** Mrs. Garcia	**5** Margarita
555–2764	555–4930	555-0217	555–1020	555-0721

❹ Practice the Conversation: Getting a Wrong Number 121

Listen to the conversation. Then listen and repeat.

A: Is Maya there?

B: No, I'm sorry. What number are you calling?

A: Is this 555–4697 ?

B: No, it isn't.

A: Sorry to bother you.

B: That's okay . Goodbye.

A: Bye.

Practice the conversation with a partner. Use these items.

1 Mr. Wu	**2** Sam Martin	**3** Lisa Jones	**4** Ms. Fallon	**5** Dr. Williams
555–4938	555–3957	555–2468	555–3000	555–0700
No problem.	That's all right.	Okay.	All right.	That's okay.

wrong number = an incorrect telephone number

Safety Resources

❶ Learn New Words 122

Look at the pictures. Listen to the words. Then listen and repeat.

① smoke detector

② carbon monoxide detector

③ fire extinguisher

④ child safety locks

⑤ safety gate

⑥ handrails

⑦ child safety seat

⑧ deadbolt lock

⑨ window guard

❷ Check

Check (✔) the things you have at home.

- ○ Smoke detector
- ○ Carbon monoxide (CO) detector
- ○ Fire extinguisher
- ○ Child safety locks
- ○ Safety gate

- ○ Handrails
- ○ Child safety seat
- ○ Deadbolt lock
- ○ Window guard

Talk with a partner. What item is the most important to you?

❸ Listen and Read 123

Listen and read the website information.

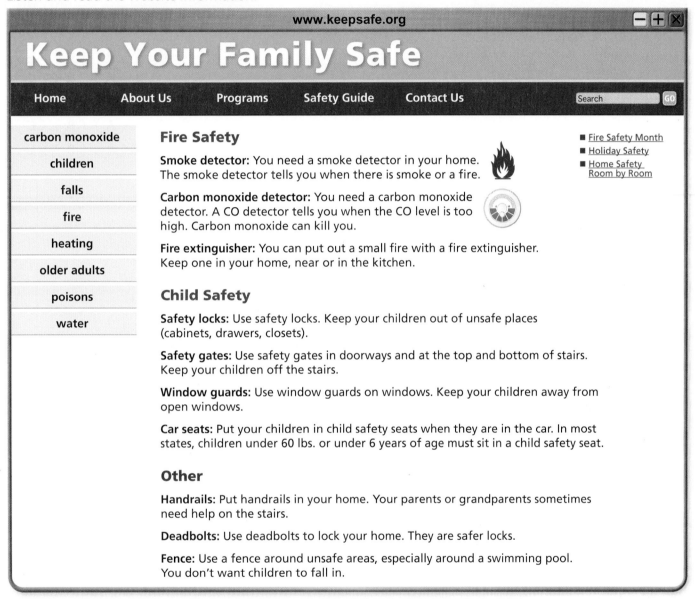

www.keepsafe.org

Keep Your Family Safe

| Home | About Us | Programs | Safety Guide | Contact Us | Search | GO |

carbon monoxide
children
falls
fire
heating
older adults
poisons
water

Fire Safety

Smoke detector: You need a smoke detector in your home. The smoke detector tells you when there is smoke or a fire.

Carbon monoxide detector: You need a carbon monoxide detector. A CO detector tells you when the CO level is too high. Carbon monoxide can kill you.

Fire extinguisher: You can put out a small fire with a fire extinguisher. Keep one in your home, near or in the kitchen.

Child Safety

Safety locks: Use safety locks. Keep your children out of unsafe places (cabinets, drawers, closets).

Safety gates: Use safety gates in doorways and at the top and bottom of stairs. Keep your children off the stairs.

Window guards: Use window guards on windows. Keep your children away from open windows.

Car seats: Put your children in child safety seats when they are in the car. In most states, children under 60 lbs. or under 6 years of age must sit in a child safety seat.

Other

Handrails: Put handrails in your home. Your parents or grandparents sometimes need help on the stairs.

Deadbolts: Use deadbolts to lock your home. They are safer locks.

Fence: Use a fence around unsafe areas, especially around a swimming pool. You don't want children to fall in.

- Fire Safety Month
- Holiday Safety
- Home Safety Room by Room

Match the family members to the safety equipment. Share your ideas with your classmates.

Equipment	Who is it for?
smoke detector _____	
safety locks _____	• children
car seat _____	• grandparents
handrail _____	• parents
safety gate _____	• everyone
fire extinguisher _____	

What Do You Know?

❶ Listening Review 124

Listen to the conversation. To finish the conversation, listen and choose the correct answer: *A*, *B*, or *C*. Use the Answer Sheet.

1. A. No, I'm sorry. She's not home.
B. What's your phone number?
C. Call Jeff at 555-7723.

2. A. I think you have the wrong number.
B. This is Maria. I'm her classmate.
C. Just a minute. I'll get her.

3. A. Yes, please. Ask him to call Dr. Smith.
B. Right. Thank you.
C. You're welcome.

4. A. He's cooking dinner.
B. I usually play soccer.
C. No, I don't.

5. A. I pay the bills.
B. I don't have a brother.
C. My parents and my sister.

Answer Sheet

1 (A) (B) (C)
2 (A) (B) (C)
3 (A) (B) (C)
4 (A) (B) (C)
5 (A) (B) (C)

❷ Dictation 125

Listen and write the questions you hear. Then write your answers.

1. _____
_____

2. _____
_____

3. _____
_____

4. _____
_____

5. _____
_____

❸ Grammar Review

Circle the correct answer: *A*, *B*, or *C*.

1. I _____ two brothers.

A. has
B. have
C. doesn't have

2. _____ he live in Morocco?

A. Do
B. Is
C. Does

3. I wash the dishes five days a week.
I _____ wash the dishes.

A. usually
B. sometimes
C. never

4. My husband takes out the trash every day.
I _____ take out the trash.

A. often
B. sometimes
C. never

5. _____ they go to school?

A. Does
B. Do
C. Are

6. I have a brother, _____ I don't have a sister.

A. but
B. or
C. and

LEARNING LOG ✔

I know these words:

- ○ afraid
- ○ angry
- ○ aunt
- ○ brother
- ○ carbon monoxide detector
- ○ child safety lock
- ○ child safety seat
- ○ children
- ○ clean the house
- ○ confused
- ○ cook dinner
- ○ cousin

- ○ dance
- ○ daughter
- ○ deadbolt lock
- ○ do the laundry
- ○ father
- ○ feed the pets
- ○ fence
- ○ fire extinguisher
- ○ fix things
- ○ go grocery shopping
- ○ granddaughter
- ○ grandfather

- ○ grandmother
- ○ grandson
- ○ handrail
- ○ happy
- ○ have picnics
- ○ husband
- ○ listen to music
- ○ make the bed
- ○ mother
- ○ nephew
- ○ never
- ○ niece
- ○ often

- ○ parents
- ○ pay the bills
- ○ play an instrument
- ○ play cards
- ○ play soccer
- ○ read the newspaper
- ○ ride a bicycle
- ○ sad
- ○ safety gate
- ○ safety lock
- ○ smoke detector
- ○ sister

- ○ sometimes
- ○ son
- ○ take out the trash
- ○ take pictures
- ○ tell stories
- ○ transportation
- ○ uncle
- ○ wash the dishes
- ○ wife
- ○ window guard

I can ask:

- ○ What's your mother's name?
- ○ Do you live with your parents?
- ○ Does he have children?
- ○ Does your family play cards?
- ○ Who's calling, please?

I can say:

- ○ I live with my wife.
- ○ My uncle's name is Andres.
- ○ No, I don't.
- ○ Yes, he does.
- ○ I usually cook dinner.
- ○ He washes the dishes.

I can write:

- ○ about my family
- ○ phone messages

Work-Out CD-ROM

Unit 7: Plug in and practice!

THINGS TO DO

❶ Learn New Words 🎧 126

Look at the picture. Listen to the words. Then listen and repeat.

* The plural of foot is feet.
** The plural of tooth is teeth.

❷ Ask Questions

Work with a partner. Point to a body part. Ask your partner to name it.

Example: A: What's this?
B: That's your leg.

❸ Practice the Conversation 🎧 127

Listen to the conversation. Then listen and repeat.

A: What's the problem?

B: My knee hurts. I can't move it.

A: Is it broken?

B: No, I don't think so.

Practice the conversation with a partner. Use the ideas below.

1 What's wrong?

2 What's the matter?

3 What's the problem?

4 Are you okay?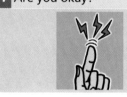

5 What's wrong?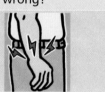

❹ Listen and Circle 🎧 128

Listen to the conversations. Circle the body part that hurts.

1. throat   shoulder   stomach
2. ear   head   eye
3. leg   neck   throat
4. knee   ankle   foot

Target Grammar
Can and *can't*
for ability   *page 181*

1 head
2 neck
3 shoulder
4 arm
5 hand
6 leg
22 finger
15 nose
14 eye
12 throat
13 tooth**
11 stomach
10 knee
8 toe
9 ankle
7 foot*
16 ear
17 mouth
18 chest
19 back
20 elbow
21 wrist

Work-Out CD-ROM
Unit 8: Plug in and practice!

At a Clinic

THINGS TO DO

❶ Learn New Words 🎧 129

Look at the picture. Listen to the words. Then listen and repeat.

① headache
② earache
③ fever
④ runny nose
⑤ cough
⑥ sore throat
⑦ backache
⑧ sprained ankle
⑨ stomachache
⑩ check-in desk
⑪ waiting room
⑫ examining room

❷ Talk about the Picture

Work with a partner. Ask about the people in the picture.

Example: *A: What's the matter with Martin's son?*
              B: He has an earache.

❸ Practice the Conversation 🎧 130

Listen to the conversation. Then listen and repeat.

A: What's the matter?

B: I have a bad headache .

A: Can you still go to school ?

B: No, I can't.

Practice the conversation with a partner. Use these items.

1 go to work

2 go to the park

3 walk

4 stand up

❹ Listen and Check 🎧 131

Listen to the sentences. Look at the picture. Check (✔) *True* or *False*.

	True	False		True	False
1.	○	○	4.	○	○
2.	○	○	5.	○	○
3.	○	○	6.	○	○

Target Grammar
Questions with *can*   page 183

LESSON 3 — Understanding Doctors' Orders

1 Drink liquids.

THINGS TO DO

❶ Learn New Words 🎧 132

Look at the pictures. Listen to the words. Then listen and repeat.

❷ Interview

Ask a partner. Look at the pictures. Complete the chart below.
More than one answer is possible.

What do you think you should do for a / an _____ ?	
earache	*Use ear drops;* _____
headache	_____
sore throat	_____
sprained ankle	_____
backache	_____

10 Keep it dry.

Share your partner's answers with the class.

Example: *My partner uses ear drops for an earache.*

❸ Practice the Conversation 🎧 133

Listen to the conversation. Then listen and repeat.

A: What's the matter?

B: I have a sore throat .

A: You should drink liquids .

B: What else should I do?

A: You should rest , too.

Practice the conversation with a partner. Use these problems.
Use the vocabulary words to respond.

  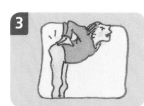

Target Grammar

Should and *shouldn't*
for advice *page 184*

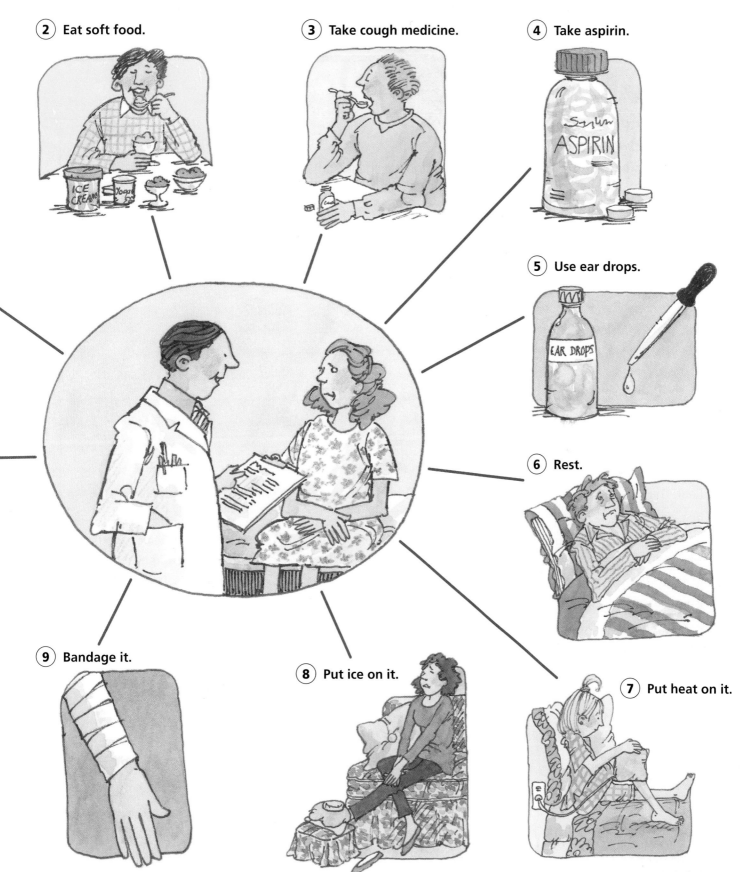

2 Eat soft food.

3 Take cough medicine.

4 Take aspirin.

ASPIRIN

5 Use ear drops.

EAR DROPS

6 Rest.

9 Bandage it.

8 Put ice on it.

7 Put heat on it.

Medicine Labels

THINGS TO DO

❶ Learn New Words 134

Look at the pictures. Listen to the words. Then listen and repeat.

❷ Read and Write

Read the information in the pictures. Then complete the information below.

Medicine	How much?	How often?	With food?
Avrocet	_____ tablets	every _____ hours	yes
Aurolite	_____ drops	every _____ hours	
All-Better Adults: Children 6–12:	_____ teaspoons _____ teaspoons	every _____ hours every _____ hours	
Adifen Adults: Children over 12:	_____ tablets _____ tablets	every _____ hours every _____ hours	
Dream-eez Adults:	_____ tablets	a night	

❸ Read and Circle

Read the information in the pictures. Then circle the correct words to complete the sentences.

1. Sara takes Avrocet for backaches / headaches.

2. She takes it with / without food.

3. Ted takes Aurolite for his sore throat / earache.

4. He takes three drops / tablets of it every four hours.

5. Martin is 11 years old. He can / can't take Adifen.

6. Lisa is 10 years old. She can / can't take All-Better Cold and Flu.

> Some medicines are not good for children to take. Read the labels carefully or ask the pharmacist.

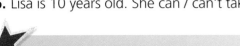

WRITING TIP
Use these words to describe how often you take something.
a   per   each   every
Example: *I take two tablets twice a day. I take them every day.*

❹ Write

Write about medicine you take. How much? How often?

Target Grammar
Object pronouns   *page 185*

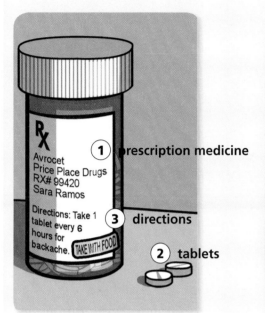

RX

Avrocet
Price Place Drugs
RX# 99420
Sara Ramos

Directions: Take 1
tablet every 6
hours for
backache. **TAKE WITH FOOD**

1 prescription medicine

3 directions

2 tablets

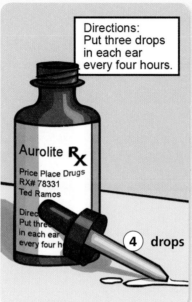

Directions:
Put three drops
in each ear
every four hours.

Aurolite **RX**

Price Place Drugs
RX# 78331
Ted Ramos

Direc...
Put three...
in each ea...
every four h...

4 drops

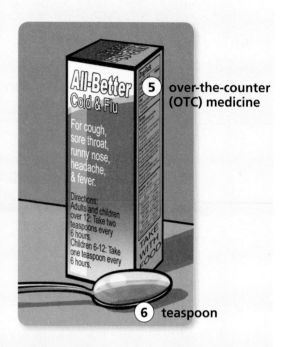

All-Better
Cold & Flu

For cough,
sore throat,
runny nose,
headache,
& fever.

Directions:
Adults and children
over 12: Take two
teaspoons every
6 hours.
Children 6-12: Take
one teaspoon every
6 hours.

TAKE WITH FOOD

5 over-the-counter
(OTC) medicine

6 teaspoon

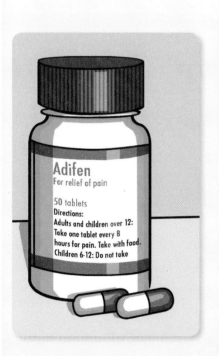

Adifen
For relief of pain

50 tablets
Directions:
Adults and children over 12:
Take one tablet every 8
hours for pain. Take with food.
Children 6-12: Do not take

Dream-eez
Take Dream-eez for
a good night's sleep!

You should not drive or use machines when
you take Dream-eez. You should sleep for
7 to 8 hours after you take it. Dream-eez
can cause headache and stomachache. If
this happens, you should call your doctor.
Dream-eez is not for children under 12.
Adults and children over 12, take one
Dream-eez before bedtime. Take on an
empty stomach.

Calling for Help

❶ Practice Pronunciation: Linking Vowel to Vowel with a *Y* or *W* Sound 135

> *I am* sounds like *Iyam*. *Who are* sounds like *whoware*.

A. Listen to the words. Then listen and repeat.

1. he is	**5.** we are	**9.** go on	**13.** she is
2. I am	**6.** try another	**10.** play it	**14.** do it
3. they are	**7.** who is	**11.** we own	**15.** day off
4. go up	**8.** who are	**12.** you are	

Write the words in the correct place.

Linking with a *y* sound	Linking with a *w* sound
he is	go on

B. Listen and complete the conversations. Then practice them with a partner. 136

1. A: This is 9-1-1.

B: My mother is hurt. _____ choking.

A: Where are you?

B: _____ at 414 Pine Street.

2. A: Where are you?

B: _____ at home.

A: How is Paul?

B: _____ resting.

❷ Learn New Words 137

Look at the pictures. Listen to the words. Then listen and repeat.

① He is choking.

② He is bleeding.

③ She is having a heart attack.

④ She is unconscious.

❸ Practice the Conversation: Calling 9-1-1 🎧 138

Listen to the conversation. Then listen and repeat.

A: This is 9-1-1.

B: We need an ambulance quickly. My friend is bleeding.

A: Where are you?

B: We are at the corner of Pine and Main.

A: The ambulance will be right there.

Practice the conversation with a partner. Use these items.

1 My father is choking. 4533 Third Street	**2** A customer is having a heart attack. Lane's Department Store, on 28th Street	**3** My mother is unconscious. 172 Eighteenth Street	**4** ? 48 Berry Avenue
Okay. The ambulance is on its way.	Someone will be there in a few minutes.	Please hold on. The ambulance is almost there.	Someone will be there soon.

❹ Practice the Conversation: Deciding What to Do 🎧 139

Listen to the conversation. Then listen and repeat.

A: What's the problem?

B: He has a bad cough. Should I call 9-1-1?

A: No. That's not an emergency.

Practice the conversation with a partner. Use these items.

1  Yes. That's an emergency.	**2**  No. That's not an emergency.	**3**  ?	**4**  ?
5 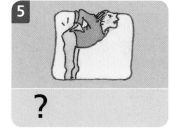 ?	**6**  ?	**7**  ?	**8** 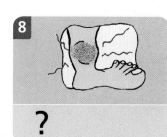 ?

LESSON 6 Safety Warnings

1 Learn New Words 🎧 140

Look at the pictures below. Listen to the words. Then listen and repeat.

① **Flammable!**

② **Poison!**

③ **Do not use if you are pregnant.**

④ **Do not take internally.**

⑤ **Do not inhale.**

⑥ **Avoid contact with skin.**

2 Read and Circle

Read the warning labels on page 113. Find and circle the vocabulary words on the labels.

3 Read and Check

Read the warning labels again. Check (✔) *True* or *False*.

	True	False
1. Pregnant women should not use fire extinguishers.	○	○
2. Paint remover is flammable.	○	○
3. It's okay to get bleach on your skin.	○	○
4. Pregnant women can use paint remover.	○	○
5. You should not inhale the contents of fire extinguishers.	○	○

4 Practice the Conversation 🎧 141

Listen to the conversation. Then listen and repeat.

A: Be careful!

B: What's wrong?

A: The warning label says, "Do not take internally."

B: Oh, thanks for warning me!

Practice the conversation with a partner. Use these items.

1 What is it?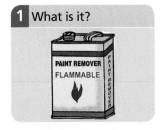

2 What's the matter?

3 Why?

4 What's wrong?

112 | **UNIT 8**

WINDOW ON MATH

Gallons, Quarts, Pints, Cups, and Ounces

1 gallon (gal.) = 4 quarts (qt.)
1 quart = 2 pints (pt.)
1 pint = 2 cups (c.) = 16 fluid ounces (fl. oz.)

| gallon | quart | pint | cup |

A Complete the sentences.

1. 2 quarts = 4 pints = __8__ cups = _____ ounces

2. 1 gallon = 4 quarts = _____ pints = _____ cups

3. 2 gallons = _____ quarts = _____ pints = _____ ounces

B Read the ads. Which bottle should you buy? Why?.

Biz Bleach
1 gallon   99¢

Biz Bleach
3 quarts   99¢

Biz Bleach
96 ounces   99¢

LESSON

7

What Do You Know?

❶ Listening Review 142

You will hear a question. Listen to the conversation. You will hear the question again. Choose the correct answer: *A*, *B*, or *C*. Use the Answer Sheet.

1. A. He can't move his ankle.
   B. His arm hurts.
   C. His wrist hurts.

2. A. He has a headache.
   B. He has a stomachache.
   C. He has an earache.

3. A. He should take aspirin and eat soft food.
   B. He should rest and use ear drops.
   C. He should rest and take aspirin.

4. A. Her brother is bleeding.
   B. Her brother isn't breathing.
   C. Her brother is at 145 Jackson Street.

5. A. He should put heat on it and take aspirin.
   B. He should put ice on it and keep it dry.
   C. He should bandage it and put ice on it.

Answer Sheet

1 Ⓐ Ⓑ Ⓒ
2 Ⓐ Ⓑ Ⓒ
3 Ⓐ Ⓑ Ⓒ
4 Ⓐ Ⓑ Ⓒ
5 Ⓐ Ⓑ Ⓒ

❷ Dictation 🎧 143

Listen and write the sentences you hear.

1. _____

2. _____

3. _____

4. _____

5. _____

114 | UNIT 8

❸ Grammar Review

Circle the correct answer: *A*, *B*, or *C*.

1. I think my leg is broken. I _____ move it.
A. should
B. can't
C. can

2. Can Ida _____ this medicine?
A. take
B. takes
C. taking

3. You need to rest. You _____ go to work today.
A. should
B. can
C. shouldn't

4. The doctor is calling _____ right now.
A. she
B. they
C. her

5. She should _____ ear drops.
A. uses
B. use
C. to use

6. Please take _____ to the doctor.
A. me
B. he
C. I

LEARNING LOG

I know these words:

○ ambulance
○ ankle
○ arm
○ aspirin
○ avoid
○ back
○ backache
○ bandage
○ bleed
○ check-in desk
○ chest
○ choke
○ contact
○ cough

○ directions
○ drink
○ drops
○ dry
○ ear
○ earache
○ elbow
○ emergency
○ examining room
○ eye
○ feet
○ fever
○ finger
○ flammable

○ foot
○ gallon
○ hand
○ head
○ headache
○ heart attack
○ heat
○ inhale
○ internally
○ knee
○ label
○ leg
○ liquids
○ medicine

○ mouth
○ neck
○ nose
○ over-the-counter
○ pint
○ poison
○ pregnant
○ prescription
○ quart
○ rest
○ runny nose
○ shoulder
○ soft food
○ sore

○ sprained ankle
○ stomach
○ stomachache
○ tablet
○ teaspoon
○ teeth
○ throat
○ toe
○ tooth
○ unconscious
○ waiting room
○ wrist

I can ask:

○ What's the matter?
○ What's this?
○ What else should I do?
○ Is it broken?

I can say:

○ Yes, I can.
○ No, I can't.
○ You should go to the doctor.
○ You shouldn't put heat on it.
○ I have a headache.

I can write:

○ advice using should or shouldn't
○ about medicine I take

Work-Out CD-ROM

Unit 8: Plug in and practice!

THINGS TO DO

❶ Learn New Words 144

Look at the pictures. Listen to the words. Then listen and repeat.

1. sofa
2. bookcase
3. lamp
4. television
5. coffee table
6. plant
7. smoke alarm
8. rug
9. mirror
10. sink
11. shower
12. toilet
13. bathtub
14. drawer
15. cabinet
16. closet
17. refrigerator
18. stove
19. dresser
20. bed

❷ Talk about the Pictures

Work with a partner. Ask and answer questions about the items below.

Example: A: *Where is the big pink rug?*
B: *It's in the living room.*

pink rug	television	smoke alarm	cabinet
refrigerator	purple chairs	green rug	small purple lamp

❸ Write

Write about the pictures.

1. There are _____closets_____ in the kitchen and the _____.

2. There is a _____ in the _____ next to the dresser.

3. The refrigerator is in the _____ next to the _____.

4. There are sinks in the _____ and the _____.

5. There are bookcases in the _____ and the _____.

6. The toilet is between the _____ and the _____.

❹ Write and Talk

Choose a room in your home. List 3 things in it. Write about the room.
Then read your sentences to the class. Your classmates can guess the room.

Example: A: *There are lamps, a dresser, and a bookcase in this room.*
B: *Is it your bedroom?*
A: *Right.*

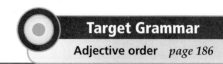

Target Grammar
Adjective order *page 186*

Living Room

Dining Room

Bathroom

Kitchen

Bedroom

Work-Out CD-ROM

Unit 9: Plug in and practice!

At Home

THINGS TO DO

① Learn New Words 145

Look at the pictures. Listen to the words. Then listen and repeat.

① porch	⑤ fence	⑨ pool
② garden	⑥ gate	⑩ carport
③ backyard	⑦ mailbox	⑪ driveway
④ garage	⑧ patio	⑫ front yard

② Listen and Check 146

Listen to the sentences. Check (✔) *Old House* or *New House*.

	Old House	New House			Old House	New House
1.	○	○		4.	○	○
2.	○	○		5.	○	○
3.	○	○		6.	○	○

③ Talk about the Pictures

Write 5 sentences about each picture. Share your ideas with a partner.

Example: *Picture A: The garden was large at the old house.*
Picture B: The children are playing basketball at the new house.

④ Compare

Make a diagram like this. Add 3 things to each part of the diagram. Then share your ideas with your classmates.

NEW HOUSE	BOTH HOUSES	OLD HOUSE
The Lees' new house has a pool.	Both houses have a driveway.	The Lees' old house was blue and white.

Which house do you like? Why?

Target Grammar

Simple past of *be*   page 187

Picture A: The Lees' Old House

Picture B: The Lees' New House

Accidents at Home: Understanding Bar Graphs

THINGS TO DO

❶ Learn New Words 🎧 147

Look at the pictures. Listen to the words. Then listen and repeat.

❷ Listen and Match 🎧 148

Look at the pictures. Listen to the conversations. Match each conversation with a person.

Conversation	Person
1. __e__	a. Joe
2. _____	b. Sylvia
3. _____	c. Carol
4. _____	d. Mike
5. _____	e. Nick
6. _____	f. Donna

❸ Practice the Conversation 🎧 149

Listen to the conversation. Then listen and repeat.

A: What happened to Joe ?

B: He fell down the stairs .

A: Is he okay now?

B: Yes, I think so.

Work with a partner. Ask about the people in the pictures.

❹ Read and Write

Read the bar graph. Answer the questions.

Questions	Answers
1. How many people got hurt when they fell down the stairs?	1,050,000
2. How many people got hurt with knives?	_____
3. How many people got hurt when they fell off chairs?	_____
4. How many people got hurt when they tripped on a rug or carpet?	_____

What happened to Joe?

① He fell down the stairs.

What happened to Donna?

⑥ She tripped on the rug.

Target Grammar

Simple past of
regular verbs   *page 189*

What happened to Sylvia?

② She fell off a ladder.

What happened to Carol?

③ She fell off a chair.

What happened to Mike?

④ He slipped in the shower.

What happened to Nick?

⑤ He cut his hand with a knife.

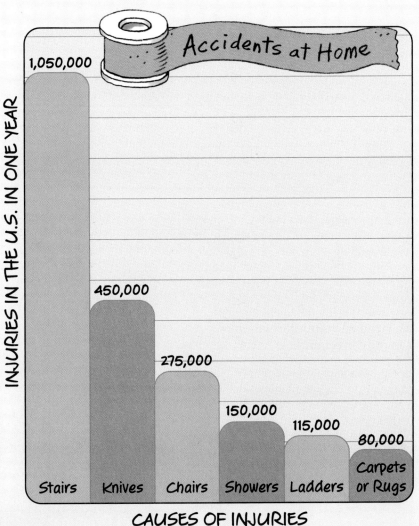

Accidents at Home

INJURIES IN THE U.S. IN ONE YEAR

1,050,000

450,000

275,000

150,000

115,000

80,000

Stairs   Knives   Chairs   Showers   Ladders   Carpets or Rugs

CAUSES OF INJURIES

Housing Ads

THINGS TO DO

❶ Learn New Words 150

Look at the pictures. Listen to the words. Then listen and repeat.

① apartment   ② condo   ③ mobile home

❷ Listen and Read 🎧 151

Listen and read the classified ads on page 123. Write the abbreviations for these words.

Word	Abbreviation	Word	Abbreviation
1. apartment	apt	4. near	
2. bathroom		5. month	
3. bedroom		6. garage	

❸ Read and Match

Read the conversations below and the ads on page 123. Match the conversations with the ads.

1. A: Would you like a place near a school?
   B: Yes, I would.   Ad: _____ b, d _____

2. A: How much would you like to pay?
   B: I would like to pay under $900 a month.   Ad: _____

3. A: How many bedrooms do you need?
   B: I need three bedrooms.   Ad: _____

4. A: What are you looking for?
   B: I would like a fireplace.   Ad: _____

5. A: Are you looking for a house or a condo?
   B: I'm looking for a condo.   Ad: _____

WRITING TIP

Before you write, brainstorm your ideas. Write all your information on
a piece of paper. Then write your ideas in the correct order.

My Ideas		
2 bathrooms	house	
$1500/month	school	
X4 bedrooms	stores	
fireplace	555-2827	

My Ad
House for Rent
4 bed, 2 bath, fireplace
nr school and stores
$1500/mo Call 555-2827

❹ Write

Write a classified ad for your dream house.

Target Grammar

Can, may, and *would like*
for requests and offers   *page 191*

REALTY

C6

SHOWCASE

a Apartment for Rent

1 bed, 1 bath
$825/mo
Call 555-9904

b Condo for Rent

2 bed, 1 bath,
gar, nr schools
patio and pool
$1100/mo
Call Bev 555-4954

c Mobile Home for Rent

2 bed, 1 bth,
patio, no pets
$875/month
call 555-9948

C9

FOR RENT

d House

3 bed/2 bath
nr schools
patio and pool
$1350/mo
Call Eileen at
555-4000

e Mobile Home

1 bed, 1 bath
nr public pool
$795/mo
Call Joe
555-1928

f Apartment

2 Br, 2 Ba apt.
pool & patio
$950/mo
Call John
555-4583

FOR SALE

g Condo

2 bed, 1.5 bath
nr stores
$175,000
Call Smith
Realty
555-6767

h House

3 BR, 2 BA,
big kitchen,
2 fireplaces,
patio, gar.
$210,000
Call Marlene
555-1200, ext.15

A 1.5 bath is a full bathroom and
a half bathroom. A half bathroom only has
a sink and a toilet.

❶ Practice Pronunciation: Stress in Compound Nouns 152

> In compound nouns the stress is usually on the first part of the word.

A. Listen to the words. Then listen and repeat.

1. <u>book</u>case	2. bedroom	3. bathroom	4. bathtub	5. mailbox
6. carport	7. fireplace	8. grandson	9. drugstore	10. headache

Underline the stress in the words.

B. Work with a partner. Ask and answer the questions. Use the words in Activity A.

1. Where can you mail letters?
2. Where can you buy medicine?
3. Where do you sleep?
4. Where do you take a shower?
5. Where can you put books?
6. Who is your daughter's son?
7. If your head hurts, what do you have?
8. Where do you put your car?
9. Where do you take a bath?
10. Where do you make a fire in your home?

❷ Practice the Conversation: Calling about a Place for Rent 153

Listen to the conversation. Then listen and repeat.

A: Hello. May I speak with Kim, please?

B: Yes, this is Kim.

A: I'm calling about the house for rent. Is it still available?

B: Yes, it is.

A: How many bedrooms does it have?

B: Three .

A: And how many bathrooms?

B: Two .

A: Okay. Thank you very much.

Practice the conversation with a partner. Use these items.

1 apartment	**2** mobile home	**3** condo	**4** house	**5** condo
Two	One	Two small ones	Four, … no, five	One large and
One and a half	One	One	Three	two small
				Two

❸ Practice the Conversation: Asking for More Information 154

Listen to the conversation. Then listen and repeat.

A: Hi, I'm calling about the house for rent. Is it still available?

B: Yes, it is.

A: Can you tell me a little more about it?

B: Sure. It has a large front yard, a patio, and a garden.

A: Thanks.

Practice the conversation with a partner. Use these items.

1 apartment
a small dining room, a small living room, and a large kitchen

2 condo
a patio, a pool, and a garden

3 mobile home
a carport, a porch, and a large front yard

4 house
a pool, a small front yard, and a garage

5 mobile home
a front yard, a backyard, and a patio

❹ Practice the Conversation: Asking about Rent 155

Listen to the conversation. Then listen and repeat.

A: How much is the rent?

B: $1,200 a month. Would you like to see it?

A: Yes, I would. How about Tuesday at 5:30?

B: Sure. I'll see you then.

Practice the conversation with a partner. Use these items.

1 $950
Friday at 2:15

2 $825
Saturday at 3:30

3 $400
Thursday at noon

4 $2,200
Wednesday at 7:00

5 $1,075
Monday at 4:45

Understanding Utilities

❶ Learn New Words 156

Look at the bills. Listen to the words. Then listen and repeat

(1) gas and electric

(2) cable

(3) bill

SOUTHERN GAS and ELECTRIC COMPANY
P.O. Box 4157
Long Beach, CA 90807-4157

Energy Statement

John Alvarez
1622 Walnut Ave.
Long Beach, CA 90807

(4) ACCOUNT NUMBER	DUE DATE
6464560483-0	02/07/12

(5) AMOUNT DUE
$ 133.19

FOR SERVICES PROVIDED TO:

6464560483-0
1622 Walnut Ave.

Bill Date   **01/12/12**

Previous Balance	**$ 132.22**
Payment	**$ 132.22**
Balance forward	**$ 0.00**

(6) AMOUNT ENCLOSED

$133.19

T&T TELEPHONE COMPANY
P.O. Box 330, Long Beach, CA 90807-0330

Customer Invoice

Account Number: 000-493-3844 979 004

Bill Period: Dec 15 – Jan 15

Sent to: John Alvarez
1622 Walnut Ave.
Long Beach, CA 90807

(7) New Charges: $ 56.29

Amount Due: **$ 56.29**

Due Date: 02/02/12

Detach Here – Return this portion with your payment.

❷ Read and Check

Read the sentences. Check (✔) *True* or *False*.

	True	False
1. John's account number with the gas and electric company is 000-493-3844 979 004.	○	○
2. John is paying the gas and electric company $132.22.	○	○
3. John's balance forward to the gas and electric company is $0.	○	○
4. John's phone bill is for December 15 to January 15.	○	○
5. John's account number with the telephone company is 6464560483-0.	○	○
6. The due date for the telephone bill is February 2.	○	○
7. John's address is P.O Box 4157, Long Beach, CA, 90807-4157.	○	○
8. John owes $56.29 to the telephone company.	○	○

❸ Write

Complete the checks. Use the bills from Activity 1.

JOHN ALVAREZ
1622 Walnut Ave.
Long Beach, CA 90807

1129

DATE_____

PAY TO THE ORDER OF _Southern Gas and Electric Company_ $ [   ]

_____ DOLLARS

FIRST NATIONAL BANK of CALIFORNIA
Los Angeles, California

MEMO_____

⑈012345678⑈:   353⑉009 2⑊ 1129

JOHN ALVAREZ
1622 Walnut Ave.
Long Beach, CA 90807

1130

DATE_____

PAY TO THE ORDER OF_____ $ [   ]

_____ DOLLARS

FIRST NATIONAL BANK of CALIFORNIA
Los Angeles, California

MEMO_____

⑈012345678⑈:   353⑉009 2⑊ 1130

What Do You Know?

➊ Listening Review 157

Listen to the conversation. To finish the conversation, listen and choose the correct answer: *A*, *B*, or *C*. Use the Answer Sheet.

1. A. Yes, it is.
   B. Yes, I would.
   C. Yes, it has two bedrooms.

2. A. It has two bedrooms.
   B. Yes, it is.
   C. It's $1,150 a month.

3. A. Is he okay?
   B. Are you okay?
   C. Would you like to see it?

4. A. Is she okay now?
   B. He tripped on the rug.
   C. She fell down the stairs.

5. A. No, it doesn't have a garage.
   B. Yes, I would like to see it.
   C. Sure, it has a big front yard, a garden, and a garage.

Answer Sheet

1 (A) (B) (C)
2 (A) (B) (C)
3 (A) (B) (C)
4 (A) (B) (C)
5 (A) (B) (C)

➋ Dictation  158

Listen and write the sentences you hear.

1. _____

2. _____

   _____

3. _____

   _____

4. _____

5. _____

❸ Grammar Review

Circle the correct answer: A, B, or C.

1. There is a _____ in the bathroom.

   A. small blue rug
   B. blue small rug
   C. rug small blue

2. Ted _____ his brother last night.

   A. call
   B. called
   C. calling

3. Anne _____ at my house yesterday.

   A. were
   B. was
   C. is

4. Can I _____ to Marta, please?

   A. talk
   B. talking
   C. to talk

5. Kim and I_____ in the garden this morning.

   A. am
   B. was
   C. were

6. I _____ to see the apartment on Monday.

   A. like
   B. would likes
   C. would like

LEARNING LOG

I know these words:

○ account number	○ cable	○ fell	○ lamp	○ rug
○ amount due	○ carpet	○ fence	○ mailbox	○ shower
○ amount enclosed	○ carport	○ fireplace	○ mirror	○ sink
○ apartment	○ closet	○ front yard	○ mobile home	○ slip
○ available	○ coffee table	○ garage	○ new charges	○ smoke alarm
○ backyard	○ condo	○ garden	○ patio	○ sofa
○ bathtub	○ cut	○ gas and electric	○ plant	○ stairs
○ bed	○ drawer	○ gate	○ pool	○ stove
○ bill	○ dresser	○ house	○ porch	○ television
○ bookcase	○ driveway	○ knife	○ refrigerator	○ toilet
○ cabinet	○ fall	○ ladder	○ rent	○ trip

I can ask:

○ What happened to Joe?
○ Does it have a yard?
○ How much is the rent?
○ Is it still available?
○ How many bedrooms does it have?
○ Can you tell me a little more about it?

I can say:

○ There is a closet in the room.
○ Our new house has a bathtub.
○ Our old house had a pool.
○ He tripped on the rug.
○ I need two bedrooms.
○ I'm looking for a condo.

I can write:

○ about my dream house
○ checks to pay bills

Work-Out CD-ROM

Unit 9: Plug in and practice!

THINGS TO DO

❶ Learn New Words 159

Look at the pictures. Listen to the words. Then listen and repeat.

❷ Write

Write 5 sentences about your friends and family.

Examples: *My husband is a mover. He lifts heavy things.*
My friend José is a truck driver. He drives
a truck.

Read your sentences to the class.

❸ Find Someone Who

Talk to your classmates. Find someone who does each thing at work. When someone answers, "Yes, I do," write the person's name. Write your own idea for the last item.

Example: *A: Do you drive a car at work?*
B: Yes, I do. / No, I don't.

Find Someone Who _____	Name
drives a car	_____
cooks	_____
lifts heavy things	_____
uses a computer	_____
takes care of sick people	_____
builds things	_____
_____	_____

❹ Listen and Match 160

Listen to the conversations. Match the jobs to the conversations.

Conversations	Jobs
1. _____	**a.** a plumber
2. _____	**b.** a home healthcare provider
3. _____	**c.** a childcare worker
4. _____	**d.** a mover
5. _____	**e.** a mechanic

Indoor Jobs

① Adam is a <u>chef</u>. He cooked food today.

② Anita is an <u>office manager</u>. She used a computer, a fax machine, and a photocopier today.

③ Sam Is a <u>plumber</u>. He repaired sinks and toilets today.

④ Julie is a <u>home healthcare provider</u>. She took care of sick people in their homes today.

Work-Out CD-ROM
Unit 10: Plug in and practice!

Indoor/Outdoor Jobs

5 Tony is a <u>childcare worker</u>.
He took care of children today.

6 Mike is a <u>mechanic</u>.
He fixed cars today.

7 Jack is a <u>mover</u>. He lifted
heavy things today.

Outdoor Jobs

8 Dan is a <u>construction worker</u>.
He built buildings today.

9 Bill is a <u>truck driver</u>. He drove
a truck today.

10 Alan is a <u>landscaper</u>. He took
care of plants today.

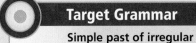

Target Grammar

Simple past of irregular
verbs   *page 192*

LESSON 2 — Understanding Forms of Identification

THINGS TO DO

❶ Learn New Words 161

Look at the documents. Listen to the words. Then listen and repeat.

❷ Read and Circle

Look at the forms of identification below. Can you use them as identification for employment? Circle *yes* or *no* for each item.

1. Certificate of graduation   yes   no
2. U.S. passport   yes   no
3. Driver's license   yes   no
4. Foreign passport without I-551 stamp   yes   no
5. Permanent Resident Card   yes   no

❸ Read and Write

Read the job ads. Take notes in the chart below.

Job	Part-time or Full-time	Benefits?
Construction worker	full-time	yes
Chef		
Office manager		
Landscaper		
Childcare worker		
Pharmacist's assistant		

❹ Practice the Conversation 162

Listen to the conversation. Then listen and repeat.

A: Can you start on Monday at 8:00 A.M.?

B: Yes. I'll be here.

A: Please bring a form of identification for employment.

B: Is an employment authorization document okay?

A: Yes, that's fine. / No, I'm sorry. That won't work.

Practice the conversation with a partner. Use these items and the correct response.

1. a foreign passport   2. a driver's license   3. a permanent resident card   4. Form I-94

① U.S. Passport

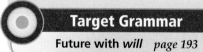

Target Grammar

Future with *will*   *page 193*

Forms of Identification for Employment

(2) **Permanent Resident Card**

(3) **Foreign passport with a temporary I-551 stamp**

(4) **Employment Authorization Document with photograph**

(5) **Form I-94 (arrival / departure record)**

Competitive Wages & Benefits

CONSTRUCTION WORKERS NEEDED
Call 860–555–3209
and leave message.
Full-time work.

Legends Grill
Immediate Opening
for Full-Time Chef
Excellent benefits
Call John for an
interview
4 Corey Drive
212–555–6948

SPS, Inc.
Has an immediate opening
for a full-time Office Manager.
Benefits include medical
insurance and paid vacation.
$20 per hour. If interested
call for an interview.
(503)555–9438

Full-Time Help Wanted
Reliable LANDSCAPERS
• Excellent Pay
• Good Benefits
Apply in Person
Spring Look Landscaping
66 River Road, Santa Anita

**Childcare Worker
Part-Time**
$12/hr.
Sorry, no benefits.
Call Judy Eno
818–555–9483

Allen's Drugstore
Pharmacist's assistant
needed. 40 hours a
week. Good benefits.
Call 430–555–3482 for
an interview.

THINGS TO DO

❶ Learn New Words 🎧 163

Look at the picture. Listen to the words. Then listen and repeat.

① job fair ③ dress neatly ⑤ interview
② chew gum ④ shake hands ⑥ résumé

❷ Talk about the Picture

Write 5 things about the picture. Then share your ideas with the class.

Example: *Fatima is having an interview.*
Scott dressed neatly for the job fair.

❸ Practice the Conversation 🎧 164

Listen to the conversation. Then listen and repeat.

A: So, tell me about yourself.

B: Well, right now I'm an office manager . I got the job in 2010 .

A: I see. And what did you do before that?

B: Before that, I was a landscaper .

Practice the conversation with a partner. Use these items.

| a childcare worker/2009 a sales clerk | a construction worker/2007 a landscaper | a nurse/2006 a pharmacist's assistant | a librarian/2008 a teacher |

❹ Listen and Take Notes 🎧 165

Listen to Rosa's job interview. Write the missing information.

Rosa Perez		
Employer	**Job Title**	**Dates**
Lane's		2008 – Present
Lane's		2004 – 2008
The Elephant's Trunk	Sales clerk	–

❺ Give Opinions

Talk with your classmates.

What should you do at a job interview? What shouldn't you do?

You should...	You shouldn't...
listen carefully	be late

ANNUAL JOB FAIR

Paul

Elisa

Tim

Target Grammar

Adverbs of manner *page 194*

An Amazing Story

THINGS TO DO

❶ Learn New Words 166

Look at the pictures. Listen to the words. Then listen and repeat. Find and circle the words in the story.

① fast-food restaurant   ③ borrowed   ⑤ improved

② promoted   ④ bad condition   ⑥ future

❷ Talk about the Pictures

Write one sentence about each picture.

Example: *The men are cleaning the car in picture 1.*

Share your sentences with the class.

❸ Listen and Read 167

Listen and read the story. Put the events in order from first (1) to last (6).

_____ He sold 1 restaurant and bought 3 more.

_____ He worked as a chef's assistant.

_____ He managed a fast-food restaurant.

_____ He owns 168 restaurants.

___1___ Mr. Kazi worked at a car rental company.

_____ He bought a restaurant.

> **WRITING TIP**
> Use time words to talk about when things happen in a story.
> *Today*   *When I was*   *A year later*

❹ Write

Complete the sentences below. Write about your jobs in order from first to last.

1. When I was _____ years old I got my first job as a _____.

2. _____ years later, I worked as a _____.

3. A few years later, I was a _____.

4. Now I am a _____.

5. In the future, I'm going to be a _____.

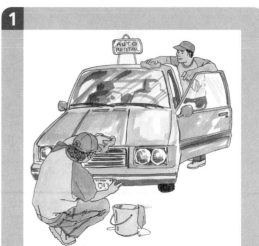

Mr. Kazi came to the United States when he was 23 years old. His first job was for a car rental company.

A few years later Mr. Kazi borrowed money from a bank. He bought a fast-food restaurant. It was in very bad condition. He repaired the building and improved the food. He worked seven days a week. Soon the restaurant was making money.

Target Grammar

Future with *be going to*   page 195

2

On weekends, Mr. Kazi worked as a chef's assistant at a fast-food restaurant. He cleaned the kitchen and helped the chef.

3

Mr. Kazi worked very hard in the restaurant. Soon the owners of the restaurant promoted him to restaurant manager. He managed the restaurant for the next three years.

5

A year later Mr. Kazi sold his restaurant. He made a lot of money. Then he bought three more restaurants.

6

Kazi's Restaurants in All 50 States!

Today Mr. Kazi is the owner of 168 restaurants. He is going to buy more restaurants in the future.

LESSON 5 — Answering Job Interview Questions

❶ Practice Pronunciation: Past Tense Endings 168

> The past tense ending -ed can sound like *t* as in *fixed*, *d* as in *repaired*, or *id* as in *repeated*.

A. Listen to the words. Listen and repeat. Then match each word to the correct ending sound.

1. lifted _____   **a.** ending sounds like t
2. cooked _____   **b.** ending sounds like d
3. used _____   **c.** ending sounds like id

B. Listen to the words. Listen and repeat. Then write the words in the correct place in the chart. 169

1. repaired	**4.** repeated	**7.** lifted	**10.** contacted	**13.** called
2. fixed	**5.** stopped	**8.** dressed	**11.** tried	**14.** cleaned
3. opened	**6.** entered	**9.** washed	**12.** walked	**15.** rented

Ending sounds like *t*	Ending sounds like *d*	Ending sounds like *id*
fixed	repaired	repeated

❷ Practice the Conversation: Talking about Work Experience  170

Listen to the conversation. Then listen and repeat.

A: Tell me about your last job.

B: Well, I worked at a department store . I was a sales clerk .

A: Did you like helping people ?

B: Yes, I liked it a lot. And the people that I worked with were very friendly.

Practice the conversation with a partner. Use these items.

1 restaurant	**2** school	**3** garage	**4** hospital
chef's assistant	childcare worker	mechanic	nurse
cooking	taking care of children	fixing cars	taking care of people

3 **Practice the Conversation: Talking about Changing Jobs** 171

Listen to the conversation. Then listen and repeat.

A: Why did you leave your last job?

B: I went back to school .

A: I see. And why do you want to work at this company ?

B: I like the people here, and you offer great benefits to employees.

Practice the conversation with a partner. Use these items.

1 The restaurant closed.	2 My family moved here.	3 I didn't have benefits.	4 I wanted to move to a new town.
restaurant	school	office	hospital

5 My child was sick.	6 My hours were cut.	7 I hurt my back.	8 It was a part-time job.
business	store	garage	library

4 **Practice the Conversation: Talking about Strengths** 172

Listen to the conversation. Then listen and repeat.

A: Why should I hire you?

B: I think you should hire me because I'm a hard worker and I work well with people .

A: That's good. We like our employees to get along with people .

B: I'm glad to hear that.

Practice the conversation with a partner. Use these items.

1 I listen carefully.	2 I have experience.	3 I'm never late.	4 I'm good at helping people.
listen carefully	have experience	be on time	be good at helping people

5 I ask questions.	6 I dress neatly.	7 I drive carefully.	8 I'm good at taking care of children.
ask questions	be neat	be careful drivers	be good with children

Completing a Job Application

❶ Read and Write

Read about Felipe Yasine. Then complete the job application below for him.

My name is Felipe Martin Yasine, and I live at 2435 Melford Avenue in Sacramento, California. In my country, I worked as a mechanic. I liked my job a lot. My friends say I'm a good mechanic. Now I don't have a job. I really want a full-time job. I can work in the mornings and afternoons on Monday through Friday. I can work in the afternoons on the weekends.

JOB APPLICATION

First Name: _____ Middle Initial: _____ Last Name: _____

Birth Date: _____ 6 / 23 / 70 _____ Phone Number: _____ (916) 555-4938 _____

Present Address: _____ .

City: _____ State: _____ Zip Code: 95652 _____

Are you currently employed?   ○ Yes   ○ No

Do you have a valid driver's license?   ☑ Yes   ○ No

Number of hours per week desired: _____

Days and A.M./P.M. hours available:

	Mon.	Tues.	Weds.	Thurs.	Fri.	Sat.	Sun.
A.M.	○	○	○	○	○	○	○
P.M.	○	○	○	○	○	○	○

List your last three jobs:

Company Name	Your Position	From	To
Green Thumb Landscapers	Manager	June 2008	September 2011
ABC Landscaping	Landscaper	April 2005	May 2008
Ruiz Auto	Mechanic	January 2000	February 2005

❷ Write

Complete this job application with information about yourself.

JOB APPLICATION

First Name: _____ Middle Initial: _____ Last Name: _____

Birth Date: _____ / _____ / _____   Phone Number: (_____) _____

Present Address: _____.

City: _____ State: _____ Zip Code: _____

Are you currently employed?   ○ Yes   ○ No

Do you have a valid driver's license?   ○ Yes   ○ No

Number of hours per week desired: _____

Days and A.M./P.M. hours available:

	Mon.	Tues.	Weds.	Thurs.	Fri.	Sat.	Sun.
A.M.	○	○	○	○	○	○	○
P.M.	○	○	○	○	○	○	○

List your last three jobs:

Company Name	Your Position	From	To

❸ Interview

Interview a classmate. Ask 5 questions about his or her job application.

Example: *A: Are you currently employed?*   *B: Yes, I am.*

WINDOW ON MATH

Word Problems

Work with a partner. Answer these word problems.

1. Sam worked 40 hours a week as a mechanic last February. He earned $20.00 an hour. How much did he earn in a month?
2. Taka earns $12.00 an hour as a childcare worker. She works Monday, Wednesday, and Friday from 7 A.M. to 4 P.M. She gets an unpaid hour for lunch each day. How much does she earn a week?
3. Robert is a chef's assistant. He works part-time in two restaurants. He works from 7 A.M. to 1 P.M. Monday through Friday and earns $10.00 an hour. He works from 4 P.M. to 11 P.M. on Saturday and Sunday and earns $15.00 an hour. How much does he earn a week?

1 Listening Review 173

Look at the pictures and listen. Choose the correct answer: *A*, *B*, or *C*.
Use the Answer Sheet.

1. A   B   C

2. A   B   C

3. A   B   C

4. A   B    C

5. A    B   C

Answer Sheet

1 (A)	(B)	(C)
2 (A)	(B)	(C)
3 (A)	(B)	(C)
4 (A)	(B)	(C)
5 (A)	(B)	(C)

2 Dictation 174

Listen and write the questions you hear.

1. _____

2. _____

3. _____

Answer the questions you wrote above.

4. _____

5. _____

6. _____

❸ Grammar Review

Circle the correct answer: *A*, *B*, or *C*.

1. I _____ to work yesterday.
   A. was
   B. go
   C. went

2. Sue dresses _____ for work.
   A. neat
   B. neatly
   C. more neat

3. Jack _____ home at noon yesterday.
   A. came
   B. come
   C. comes

4. Ann _____ have a job interview next week.
   A. going to
   B. is going to
   C. is going

5. I _____ you to work tomorrow.
   A. drive
   B. am drive
   C. will drive

6. _____ going to fill out the application?
   A. Are you
   B. Are
   C. You are

LEARNING LOG

I know these words:

- ○ assistant
- ○ authorization
- ○ benefits
- ○ borrow
- ○ build
- ○ chef
- ○ chew gum
- ○ childcare worker
- ○ condition
- ○ construction worker

- ○ cook
- ○ document
- ○ dress neatly
- ○ drive
- ○ driver's license
- ○ employment
- ○ fast-food restaurant
- ○ fax machine
- ○ foreign
- ○ future

- ○ heavy
- ○ hire
- ○ home healthcare provider
- ○ identification
- ○ improve
- ○ indoor
- ○ interview
- ○ job fair
- ○ landscaper
- ○ lift

- ○ listen carefully
- ○ mechanic
- ○ mover
- ○ office manager
- ○ outdoor
- ○ passport
- ○ permanent
- ○ photocopier
- ○ plumber
- ○ promoted

- ○ repair
- ○ résumé
- ○ resident
- ○ shake hands
- ○ take care of
- ○ truck driver

I can ask:

- ○ Do you use a computer at work?
- ○ Did you like your job?
- ○ Do you have experience?
- ○ Why do you want to work here?
- ○ Why did you leave your last job?
- ○ Why should I hire you?

I can say:

- ○ Right now I'm an office manager.
- ○ I was a plumber.
- ○ You shouldn't be late.
- ○ I'm going to look for a new job.
- ○ He fixed cars today.
- ○ I listen carefully.

I can write:

- ○ a job application

Work-Out CD ROM

Unit 10: Plug in and practice!

UNIT 1 GETTING STARTED

LESSON 1 Simple Present of *Be* pages 4–5

Simple Present of *Be*, Statements		
I	am	
You	are	
He		
She	is	from Haiti.
It		
We		
You	are	
They		

1 Write *am*, *is*, or *are*.

1. Salma Hayek _____is_____ from Mexico.

2. Simon Cowell and Naomi Campbell _____ from England.

3. Jackie Chan _____ from Hong Kong.

4. Yao Ming and Sun Ming Ming _____ from China.

5. Nicole Kidman and Hugh Jackman _____ from Australia.

6. Antonio Banderas _____ from Spain.

7. Shakira _____ from Colombia.

8. I _____ from _____.

2 Match the cities and countries. Then write 4 sentences.

Cities

1. _c_ Bogotá and Cali

2. ____ Beijing

3. ____ Mexico City and Durango

4. ____ San Salvador

Countries

a. in Mexico

b. in El Salvador

c. in Colombia

d. in China

Example: New York and Chicago are in the United States.

1. _____

2. _____

3. _____

4. _____

Simple Present of *Be*, Contractions

I'm		I'm = I am
You're		she's = she is
He's		he's = he is
She's	from Mexico.	it's = it is
It's		we're = we are
We're		you're = you are
You're		they're = they are
They're		

❸ Complete the conversations. Use contractions.

1. A: Hi Gina. Where are you from?

   B: _____I'm_____ from Mexico.

2. A: Where is Ms. Adams from?

   B: _____ from the United States.

3. A: My friends Marc and Ana are here.

   B: Really? Where are they from?

   A: _____ from Haiti.

4. A: Hello. My name's Tam. _____ from Vietnam.

   B: Nice to meet you, Tam. My name is Ju and this is Heejin. _____ from Korea.

5. A: Where is your ESL class?

   B: _____ in Room 101.

6. A: Mr. Jones is our teacher.

   B: Where is he from?

   A: _____ from Canada.

7. A: Hi, Said. I'm Yee.

   B: _____ from China, right?

   A: Yes, I am.

8. A: Where are Toronto and Montreal?

   B: _____ in Canada.

9. A: Where is Rio de Janeiro?

   B: _____ in Brazil.

Simple Present of *Be*, Negative Statements

I	am			Contractions
You	are			I am not = I'm not
He				she is not = she isn't
She	is	not	from Somalia.	he is not = he isn't
It				it is not = it isn't
We				we are not = we aren't
You	are			you are not = you aren't
They				they are not = they aren't

4 **Complete the sentences with the negative form. Use contractions.**

1. I _____ from China. I'm from Vietnam.

2. She _____ a student. She's the teacher.

3. Sonia and Ana _____ from Colombia. They're from Brazil.

4. My name _____ Victor. My name's Hector.

5. You _____ from Morocco. You're from Somalia.

6. We _____ from Russia. We're from France.

7. Montreal _____ in the United States. It's in Canada.

8. He _____ Duc Tran. He's Wei Lee.

5 **Look at the pictures. Write *is*, *isn't*, *are*, or *aren't*.**

Luan Nguyen
Vietnam

Amina and Musa Awad
Somalia

1. Luan _____is_____ from Vietnam. He _____ from Morocco. His last name _____ Nguyen. His last name _____ Abadi.

2. Amina and Musa _____ from China. They _____ from Somalia. Their last name _____ Awad .

Write about you.

I _____ from _____. I _____ from the United States.
My name _____. My name _____ Mary Smith.

Prepositions of Place

in	on	above	under	beside
Where's my book?	Where's the board?	Where's the map?	Where's the pencil?	Where's Sara?
It's **in** your desk.	It's **on** the wall.	It's **above** the board.	It's **under** the chair.	She's **beside** Jane.

A

B

1 Look at Picture A. Complete the sentences.

1. The map is _____on_____ the wall.
2. The clock is _____ the map.
3. The book is _____ the notebook.
4. The pen and pencil are _____ the notebook.
5. The desk is _____ the wall.
6. The student is _____ the classroom.

2 Look at Picture B. Answer the questions. Then ask and answer the questions with a partner.

1. Where is Tonya? _____
2. Where are the books? _____
3. Where are the pieces of paper? _____
4. Where is the pencil? _____
5. Where is the table? _____

Singular and Plural Nouns pages 8–9

Singular and Plural Nouns			
one **map**	two **maps**	one **book**	two **books**
one **page**	two **pages**	one **piece** of paper	two **pieces** of paper
one **country**	two **countries**	one **class**	two **classes**

1 Look at the picture. Complete the sentences. Use the singular or plural form of the words in the box.

~~board~~	chair
computer	pen
student	piece of paper

1. The _____board_____ is on the wall.

2. Three _____ are on the tables.

3. Two _____ are on a table.

4. Two _____ are in the classroom.

5. Three _____ are on the floor.

6. The _____ is under the table.

2 Write sentences about things in your classroom. Use singular and plural nouns.

1. _____Ten students are in the classroom._____

2. _____

3. _____

4. _____

5. _____

6. _____

7. _____

8. _____

Possessive Adjectives pages 10–11

Possessive Adjectives

My			Subject Pronouns	Possessive Adjectives
Your			I	my
His			you	your
Her		address is 25 Main Street.	he	his
Its			she	her
			it	its
Our			we	our
Your			you	your
Their			they	their

1 Complete the sentences with the correct possessive adjective.

1. I am from Somalia. _____My_____ name is Karim.

2. She is a student. _____ name is Adriana.

3. Ann and Tom are married. _____ last name is Bush.

4. It's nice to meet you, Lilia. What's _____ last name?

5. My name is Irina and this is Alex. We're married. _____ telephone number is 555-4599.

6. This is Paul. _____ last name is Compton.

7. Hi, Linda and Ben. What is _____ address?

8. I'm not married. _____ marital status is divorced.

2 Complete the conversations with possessive adjectives and pronouns. Then practice the conversations with a partner.

1. A: Mark and Sara are from France.

   B: What are _____ occupations?

   A: Right now, _____ are students.

2. A: Hi, I'm from Brazil. _____ name is Rosa.

   B: Hi, Rosa. _____ 'm Yusuf. What's _____ last name?

3. A: Are _____ from the United States?

   B: No, _____ am from Mexico. But _____ birthplace is Colombia.

   A: That's interesting.

4. A: Where's the teacher, Mr. Carter?

   B: _____ is in the classroom.

   A: Where are _____ students?

   B: _____ are in the classroom, too.

TARGET GRAMMAR: UNIT 1 149

Simple Present of Be, Wh- Questions

Singular Questions			Answers	Plural Questions			Answers
What	is	your name?	Tammy.	What	are	your names?	Bob and Joe.
Where		the school?	On Oak St.	Where		the students?	At school.
When		our class?	At 4:00 P.M.	When		our classes?	On Mondays and Fridays.

❶ Match the questions and answers.

1. ____g____ Where is the post office?
2. _____ What's the phone number?
3. _____ When are your classes?
4. _____ What are your occupations?
5. _____ Where are the students?
6. _____ When is his birthday?
7. _____ Where are you from?

a. They're on Tuesdays and Wednesdays.
b. It's December 5th.
c. I'm a student and my husband is a machinist.
d. 555-1945
e. I'm from Poland.
f. They're in the library.
g. It's on Pine Street.

❷ Complete the conversations. Then practice with a partner.

1. A: _____When_____ is registration?
   B: It's on Friday.

2. A: _____ are the chairs?
   B: They're in Room 102.

3. A: _____ is your telephone number?
   B: 555-1004.

4. A: _____ is Sacramento?
   B: It's in California.

5. A: _____ is the capital of Georgia?
   B: Atlanta.

6. A: _____ is Arnold Schwarzenegger from?
   B: He's from Austria.

7. A: _____ are your parties?
   B: On Friday and Saturday.

8. A: _____ is his occupation?
   B: He's a nurse.

3 **Unscramble the words to make questions. Write your answers. Then practice with a partner.**

1. first name / is / What / your / ?

_____

Your answer: _____

2. are / Where / your books / ?

_____

Your answer: _____

3. is / When / your English class / ?

_____

Your answer: _____

4. your birthplace / is / What / ?

_____

Your answer: _____

5. Where / your supermarket / is / ?

_____

Your answer: _____

6. the name / is / What / of your school / ?

_____

Your answer: _____

7. your birthday / is / When / ?

_____

Your answer: _____

8. is / What / your last name / ?

_____

Your answer: _____

9. your school / Where / is / ?

_____

Your answer: _____

10. are / Where / you from / ?

_____

Your answer: _____

Prepositions of Place

across from	between	next to
Where's the park?	Where's the post office?	Where's the fire station?
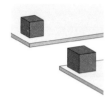		
It's **across from** the school.	It's **between** the school and the bank.	It's **next to** the police station.
in front of	**in back of**	**on the corner of**
Where's the phone?	Where's the supermarket?	Where's the hospital?

It's **in front of** the supermarket.	It's **in back of** the gas station.	It's **on the corner of** Main Street and 2nd street.

❶ Look at the picture. Complete the sentences.

1. The movie theater is _____next to_____ the restaurant.

2. The park is _____ the hospital.

3. The drugstore is _____ the hospital and the supermarket.

4. The playground is _____ the school.

5. The hospital is _____ Main Street and 2nd Street.

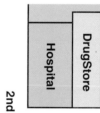
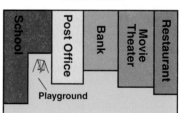

Park — 2nd Street — Hospital — DrugStore — Supermarket — Library — 1st Street — Main Street — School — Post Office — Bank — Movie Theater — Restaurant — Playground

❷ Look at the picture. Complete the conversations. Use sentences.

1. A: Where's the bank? B: It's _____

2. A: Where's the library? B: _____

3. A: What is in front of the playground? B: _____

4. A: What is next to the restaurant? B: _____

There is / There are   pages 22–23

There is / There are		
There	**is**	a supermarket on High Street.
	are	<u>two</u> supermarke<u>ts</u> on Main Street.

there is = there's

1 Look at the map. Complete the sentences. Use *there is* or *there are* and a number. Add an *s* to plural nouns.

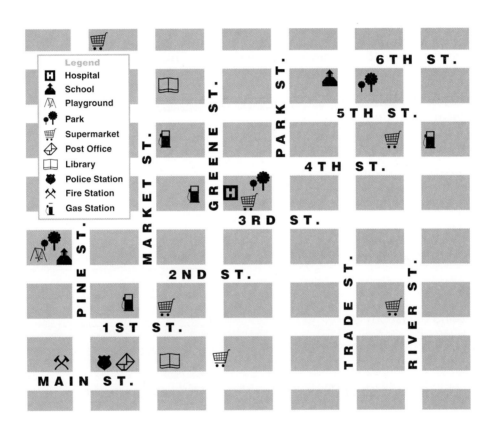

1. __There are two__ school<u>s</u>.

2. _____ hospital__.

3. _____ supermarket__.

4. _____ post office__.

5. _____ police station__.

6. _____ fire station__.

7. _____ park__.

8. _____ gas station__.

9. _____ playground__.

10. _____ librar__. (*y* or *ies*)

Questions with *Is there* / *Are there*

	Questions			Answers					
Is	there	a park on High Street?	Yes,	there	is.	No,	there	isn't.
Are		park<u>s</u> in town?			are.			aren't.

isn't = is not
aren't = are not

2 Look at the map on page 153. Answer the questions. Then practice with a partner.

1. Is there a supermarket on 3rd Street? _____Yes, there is._____

2. Are there three hospitals in Center City? _____

3. Are there two schools? _____

4. Is there a police station next to the post office? _____

5. Is there a school across from a park? _____

6. Is there a park behind the fire station? _____

7. Are there five supermarkets in Center City? _____

8. Are there four libraries? _____

9. Is there a playground on 1st Street? _____

10. Is there a library across from the post office? _____

3 Complete the questions with *Is there* or *Are there*. Then ask a partner.

1. _____ a supermarket on your street?

2. _____ a school in your town?

3. _____ two post offices in your town?

4. _____ a bank across from your home?

5. _____ good restaurants in your town?

6. _____ two movie theaters on your street?

7. _____ a library in your town?

8. _____ a park on your street?

Capitalization and Punctuation pages 24–25

		Examples
Statements	We use a **capital letter** at the beginning of a statement. We use a **period** at the end.	The movie theater is downtown. They are at school.
Questions	We use a **capital letter** at the beginning of a question. We use a **question mark** at the end.	Is there a movie theater downtown? Where are the schools?

1 **Rewrite the sentences and questions. Use capital letters, periods, and question marks.**

1. my birthday is on August 26th

    My birthday is on August 26th.

2. where are you from

_____

3. is there a bank on your street

_____

4. there is a post office in town

_____

5. the park is next to the hospital

_____

6. what is your teacher's name

_____

7. she's a teacher

_____

8. what is your last name

_____

9. my husband is from Mexico

_____

Simple Present of *Be, Yes/No* Questions

Questions				Answers				
Am	I			I	am.		I	'm not
Are	you			you	are.		you	aren't.
Is	he she it	at home?	Yes,	he she it	is.	No,	he she it	isn't.
Are	we you they			we you they	are.		we you they	aren't.

1 Match the questions and answers.

Questions	Answers
1. __*d*__ Is it 11:00?	a. No, I'm not. I'm from Guatemala.
2. _____ Are you from Mexico?	b. No, we aren't. We are on the corner of Oak Street and Pine Street.
3. _____ Is the supermarket closed?	c. Yes, he is.
4. _____ Are your classmates in the library?	~~d.~~ No, it's not. It's noon.
5. _____ Is he a student?	e. Yes, they are.
6. _____ Are you on Elm Street?	f. No, it's not. It's open.
7. _____ Am I in your class?	g. Yes, she is.
8. _____ Is she your teacher?	h. Yes, you are.

2 Read the story and answer the questions.

My name is Linda. My city is great. There are many libraries. They are open every day from 9:00 in the morning to 9:00 at night. There are many parks. They are open on Saturdays and Sundays. There is a coffee shop across from my house. It is open Monday through Saturday from noon to midnight. There is a good Korean restaurant. It is next to my school. It is open in the evenings. There is a supermarket in back of my house. It is open Monday through Friday, from 6:00 A.M. to 9:00 P.M.

1. Are the libraries open on Sunday? _____Yes, they are._____
2. Are the parks open on the weekend? _____
3. Is the coffee shop across from Linda's house? _____
4. Is the coffee shop open at night? _____
5. Is the supermarket in front of her house? _____
6. Is the Korean restaurant open in the morning? _____
7. Are the libraries open at 10:00 P.M.? _____
8. Are the parks open on Mondays? _____

❸ Unscramble the words to make questions.

1. he / Is / at the library / ?
   _____Is he at the library?_____
2. open on Monday / they / Are / ?

   _____
3. at school / Am / I / ?

   _____
4. she / at the bank / Is / ?

   _____
5. closed / it / Is / ?

   _____
6. Are / at home / you / ?

   _____

❹ Complete the questions. Then answer the questions about you and your city.

1. ____Is____ the library on your street? _____
2. _____ the restaurants open on Sundays? _____
3. _____ the supermarkets open 24 hours? _____
4. _____ the banks open on Saturday? _____
5. _____ the drugstore next to the supermarket? _____
6. _____ your school next to a park? _____
7. _____ your house across from a restaurant? _____
8. _____ your English classes on Tuesday? _____

LESSON 3 ★ Questions with *How much* and *How many* pages 36–37

Questions with *How Much* and *How Many*					
Questions					**Answers**
To ask about price	How much	is	the **book**? it?		It's five dollars. Five dollars
		are	the **tables**? **they**? **a pen and pencil**?		They're forty dollars. Forty dollars. Ninety cents.
To ask about number	How many computers How many books How many	are	there?		There **is one**. There **are seven**. Seven.

1 Write *is* or *are*.

1. How much _____ the tables?

2. How much _____ a pencil?

3. How much _____ a book and a notebook?

4. How much _____ a computer?

5. How much _____ the chairs?

6. How much _____ the clock?

7. How much _____ a calendar and a pen?

8. How much _____ the desks?

2 Write *much* or *many*.

1. A: How _____ is a notebook?
   B: $2.50.

2. A: How _____ books are there?
   B: Three.

3. A: How _____ is the pen?
   B: $1.50.

4. A: How _____ is a clock?
   B: $12.00.

5. A: How _____ pencils are there?
   B: 35.

6. A: How _____ are they?
   B: $3.00.

7. A: How _____ are there?
   B: 12.

8. A: How _____ is it?
   B: $15.00.

158 TARGET GRAMMAR: UNIT 3

③ Complete the conversations. Then practice with a partner.

```
╔══════════════════════════╗
║      Furniture Sale      ║
║  2 Tables ............. $75  ║
║  3 Chairs............. $60   ║
║  Desk .................. $35  ║
║  Couch............... $100   ║
║  2 Bookcases......... $80   ║
║  Computer Table ...... $90  ║
║  TV Stand............. $50   ║
║  Bed .................. $85   ║
╚══════════════════════════╝
```

1. A: <u>How much is the desk</u> _____? (desk)

   B: It's thirty-five dollars.

2. A: <u>How many bookcases are there</u> _____? (bookcase)

   B: There are two.

3. A: _____? (bed)

   B: It's eighty-five dollars.

4. A: _____? (table)

   B: There are two.

5. A: _____? (computer table)

   B: It's ninety dollars.

6. A: _____? (chair)

   B: They are sixty dollars.

7. A: _____? (TV stand)

   B: It's fifty dollars.

8. A: _____? (couch)

   B: It's one hundred dollars.

9. A: _____? (chair)

   B: There are three.

10. A: _____? (bed)

   B: There is one.

LESSON 4

Capitalization with Proper Nouns pages 38–39

Capitalization with Proper Nouns	
Proper nouns begin with a **capital** letter.	
Names of people	Tina Brown, Paul Lewis
Titles before names	Mr. Lewis, Mrs. Lewis, Ms. Brown, Dr. Hyde, President Lincoln
Names of countries, states, cities, oceans, rivers, lakes, nationalities	Mexico, California, Boston, Atlantic Ocean, Amazon River, Lake Titicaca, Brazilian

1 **Rewrite the sentences using capital letters.**

1. i am from lima, peru.

_____

2. the capital of florida is tallahassee.

_____

3. there are two large cities in texas: dallas and houston.

_____

4. george washington was the first president of the united states.

_____

5. president barack obama is the 44th u.s. president. his mother was american. his father was from kenya.

_____

_____

2 **Answer the questions in complete sentences.**

1. What is the capital of the United States?

_____

2. What countries are next to the United States?

_____

3. What is your teacher's name?

_____

4. Where are you from?

_____

5. What nationality are you?

_____

Possessive Nouns		
		Examples
Singular Nouns	add 's	Tom → Tom's birthday. Susie → Susie's birthday. Barbara → Barbara's car. Francis → Francis's party.
Plural Nouns	add '	the students → the students' books the boys → the boys' games

1 **Complete the sentences with possessive nouns. Use the nouns in parentheses.**

1. _____Bob's_____ game is on Sunday, August 2. (Bob)

2. When are the _____ dental appointments? (girls)

3. _____ PTA meeting is on Wednesday. (Lois)

4. _____ doctor's appointment is at 11:30 in the morning. (Pat)

5. When is _____ birthday party? (Anne)

6. The _____ basketball game is on Saturday. (boys)

7. _____ job interview is at 2:00 in the afternoon. (Iris)

8. The _____ party is on Wednesday, October 4. (class)

9. When is _____ haircut? (Maria)

10. The _____ party is on Friday. (students)

2 **Correct the mistakes in the possessive nouns.**

1. When is Martins' job interview? _____Martin's_____

2. Iris computer class is on Saturday. _____

3. The girls basketball games are on Wednesday. _____

4. Where is Tims basketball game? _____

5. Lois birthday is this Friday. _____

6. What date is Billys' doctors appointment? _____

7. When is Annes' meeting? _____

8. The boy's schools are closed today. _____

Prepositions of Time pages 50–51

Prepositions of Time

Prepositions	Use	Examples
in	parts of the day months seasons years	The appointment is **in** the morning. My birthday is **in** September. The holiday is **in** the spring. The Olympic Games are **in** 2016.
on	days dates	The class is **on** Friday. The interview is **on** January 10th.
at	times of the day night	The test begins **at** 4:00. Our class is **at** night.

1 **Complete the sentences. Use *in, on,* or *at*.**

1. My birthday is ____on____ Tuesday.
2. Maria's class begins _____ 9:30 _____ the morning.
3. The appointment is _____ 2:00 _____ the afternoon.
4. The swim classes are _____ the summer.
5. The English test is _____ May 1st.
6. The party is _____ 8:00 _____ night.
7. The bank is closed _____ Sundays.
8. My brother's birthday is _____ June.
9. The basketball game is _____ night.
10. The Olympic Games are _____ 2012.

2 **Read the sentences and find the mistakes. Rewrite the sentences.**

1. My dental appointment is at Monday. ___My dental appointment is on Monday.___
2. The computer class is on 10:00. _____.
3. The PTA meeting is at February 10th. _____.
4. Susan's birthday party is on May. _____.
5. The party is in night. _____.
6. The holiday is at the winter. _____.
7. The test is at the morning. _____.
8. His birthday is in July 5th. _____.

3 Look at the calendar and answer the questions.

January–Chris's Calendar						
Sunday	Monday	Tuesday	Wednesday	Thursday	Friday	Saturday
⑱ Basketball game 11:00 A.M.	⑲ PTA meeting 6 P.M.	⑳ English class 6:30 P.M.	㉑ Basketball game 7:30 P.M.	㉒ English class 6:30 P.M.	㉓ Job interview 9:00 A.M.	㉔ Haircut 4:00 P.M.
㉕ Basketball game 11:00 A.M.	㉖ Dental appointment 10:15 A.M.	㉗ English class 6:30 P.M	㉘ Doctor's appointment 3:30 P.M.	㉙ English class 6:30 P.M.	㉚ English class party 7:00 P.M.	㉛ Tom's birthday party 5:00 P.M.

1. When is Chris's English class? <u>*Chris's English class is on Tuesdays and Thursdays.*</u>

2. What time is Chris's English class? _____

3. When are Chris's basketball games? _____

4. When is Chris's doctor's appointment? _____

5. What time is Tom's birthday party? _____

6. When is Chris's dental appointment? _____

7. When is Chris's job interview? _____

8. What time is his haircut? _____

4 Complete the paragraph. Use *in, on,* or *at.*

Rachel is busy ____*on*____ Monday, Tuesday and Wednesday this week. Her doctor's appointment is _____ Monday _____ 9:15 _____ the morning. Her haircut is _____ 2:00 _____ the afternoon. Then, her PTA meeting is _____ 6:00 _____ night. Rachel's dental appointment is _____ Tuesday _____ 10:45 _____ the morning. Her computer class is _____ 3:00 _____ the afternoon. Then her basketball game is _____ 8:00 _____ night. Rachel's job interview is _____ Wednesday _____ 10:00 _____ the morning. Then, her computer class is _____ 1:00 _____ the afternoon. Rachel's birthday is _____ April and there is a birthday party for her _____ 7:30 _____ the evening _____ April 20. Rachel is always busy _____ the spring.

Adjective + Noun pages 52–53

Adjective + Noun				
Adjective		**Noun**		**Example**
big	good	desk	teacher	It's a **big desk.**
fun	windy	holiday	day	It's an **old computer.**
old	rainy	computer	weather	She's a **good teacher.**

1 Look at the picture. Write sentences about the picture. Use the adjectives in the box in Activity 2.

It's a ___sunny___ day at Lake Park. Lake Park is a _____ park. There are four people at the park
        (1)   (2)

today. The people are hot! It's a _____ day! It's also a _____ day. There is a woman with
                                        (3)   (4)

a kite. There are two girls with a _____ ball. There is one boy with a _____ ball. There is
                                        (5)   (6)

an _____ bicycle under a _____ tree.
        (7)   (8)

2 Match adjectives and nouns. Write 8 sentences.

Adjectives					Nouns			
pretty	ugly	big	small	bad	school	movie theater	park	bank
rainy	sunny	hot	cold	fun	desk	computer	book	chair
windy	large	new	good	old	party	meeting	day	holiday

1. ___It's an old movie theater.___

2. _____

3. _____

4. _____

5. _____

6. _____

7. _____

8. _____

Present Continuous, Statements

Statements				Negative Statements			
I	am			I	'm not		
You	are			You	aren't		
He	is	**wearing**	boots.	He	isn't	**wearing**	shoes.
She		**studying**	English.	She		**studying**	English.
We				We			
You	are			You	aren't		
They				They			

1 **Complete the sentences. Write _am, is, are, 'm not, isn't_, or _aren't_.**

1. Juan _____is_____ wearing shorts and a T-shirt today.

2. The boys _____ wearing boots. They aren't wearing running shoes.

3. My sister and I _____ wearing dresses to the party. We're wearing pants.

4. My teacher _____ wearing pants. She's wearing a skirt.

5. I _____ studying biology.

6. The student is listening. She _____ talking.

7. You are cold. You _____ wearing a sweater.

8. I _____ wearing a jacket. I'm wearing a coat.

2 **Write 6 sentences about the man in the picture.**

Example: <u>He is wearing a green hat.</u>

1. _____

2. _____

3. _____

4. _____

5. _____

6. _____

③ **Complete the conversations. Use the words in parentheses. Then practice with a partner.**

1. A: What is Maya wearing?

   B: _She's wearing a yellow dress._ (a yellow dress)

2. A: What is Jon wearing?

   B: _____ (a black suit)

3. A: What are Christine and Will wearing?

   B: _____ (hats)

4. A: What is Randy studying?

   B: _____ (math)

5. A: What are Alyssa and Ricardo eating?

   B: _____ (tacos)

6. A: What are you buying?

   B: _____ (new shoes)

④ **Write sentences about what your classmates are wearing.**

Example: _Jorge is wearing a yellow shirt._

1. _____
2. _____
3. _____
4. _____
5. _____
6. _____
7. _____
8. _____

Present Continuous, Questions

Questions				Answers					
Am	I			I	am.		I	'm not.	
Are	you			you	are.		you	aren't.	
Is	he she	**wearing** boots? **studying** math?	Yes,	he she	is.	No,	he she	isn't.	
Are	we you they			we you they	are.		we you they	aren't.	

1 **Finish the questions. Then write the answers.**

1. A: _____Is he talking_____ (he / talk) to the customer service attendant?

   B: _____Yes, he is._____ (yes)

2. A: _____ (she /come) into the store?

   B: _____ (no)

3. A: _____ (they / try) on shoes?

   B: _____ (yes)

4. A: _____ (Marie / leave) the restaurant?

   B: _____ (no)

5. A: _____ (Anne / help) a customer?

   B: _____ (no)

6. A: _____ (you / try) on hats?

   B: _____ (yes)

7. A: _____ (Kim and Bill / buy) coats?

   B: _____ (no)

8. A: _____ (we / leave) the store?

   B: _____ (yes)

9. A: _____ (you / wear) a dress?

   B: _____ (no)

10. A: _____ (George / talk) to a customer?

    B: _____ (yes)

Demonstratives: *this, that, these, those* pages 64–65

Demonstratives: *this, that, these, those*			
Singular		**Plural**	
this hat	**that** hat	**these** hats	**those** hats

1 **Complete the conversations. Use** *this, that, these* **or** *those.*

1. A: How much is <u> that sweater </u>?
   B: It's $20.

2. A: How much are _____?
   B: They're $15 each.

3. A: How much are _____?
   B: They're $10 each.

4. A: How much is _____?
   B: It's $35.

5. A: How much is _____?
   B: It's $40.

2 **Work with a partner. Point to things or people in your classroom. Say what color they are. Make sentences using** *this, that, these* **or** *those.*

Examples: 1. *This notebook is green.*
                   2. *Those books are red.*

		Examples	
a	We use **a** before a singular noun that starts with a consonant or consonant sound.	**a** <u>s</u>hirt **a** <u>c</u>ashier	**a** <u>fi</u>tting room **a** <u>u</u>niversity
an	We use **an** before a singular noun that starts with a vowel or vowel sound.	**an** <u>a</u>ttendant **an** <u>e</u>levator	**an** <u>e</u>ntrance **an** <u>h</u>our

Articles: *a* and *an*

❶ Complete the sentences. Use *a* or *an*.

1. I am going to _____*a*_____ meeting.

2. She's wearing _____ jacket and _____ hat.

3. I'm looking for _____ fitting room.

4. Is there _____ elevator in the store?

5. I'm buying _____ dress and _____ skirt.

6. Is there _____ cashier at this register?

7. Is there _____ attendant for the dressing room?

8. She is helping _____ customer.

9. I'm wearing _____ undershirt, _____ shirt and _____ sweater.

10. There is _____ entrance on Fifth Avenue and _____ entrance on King Street.

11. My teacher is wearing _____ brown skirt and _____ orange shirt.

12. I'm looking for _____ exit.

❷ Answer the questions. Use *a* or *an* in your answers.

1. What are you wearing?

_____

2. What is your teacher wearing?

_____

3. What is in your bag?

_____

Simple Present, Statements

			Irregular 3rd Person Singular Spelling
I You	work		I **go** to school. → He go**es** to school.
He She It	works	in a hospital.	I stud**y** math. → He stud**ies** math.
We You They	work		I **do** the laundry. → She do**es** the laundry. I wa**sh** the dishes. → He wash**es** the dishes.

1 Complete the sentences with the correct form of the verb in parentheses.

1. Hugo _____works_____ on Tuesdays. (work)

2. Hugo and Rosa _____ soccer on Sunday. (play)

3. Tom _____ to English class on Monday. (go)

4. Lisa _____ at the library every Wednesday. (study)

5. Tina _____ food on Friday (buy).

6. You _____ basketball on Saturdays. (play).

7. Bill and Candace are married. They _____ in Los Angeles. (live)

8. Lena _____ in an office. (work)

9. He _____ work at 6:00 P.M. (leave)

10. They _____ work in the morning. (leave)

2 Work with a partner. Write sentences about your lives. Use the verbs in the chart.

	Me	My Partner
play soccer	I play soccer on Saturdays.	Chris plays soccer on Tuesdays.
work		
live		
go to class		
buy groceries		
study		
eat breakfast		

Simple Present, Negative Statements

I You	don't		
He She	doesn't	**work**	in a library.
We You They	don't		

> don't = do not
> doesn't = does not

❸ Complete the sentences. Write *don't* or *doesn't*.

1. Hector lives with Tony. He _____*doesn't*_____ live with me.

2. We eat a lot of rice. We _____ eat a lot of bread.

3. I go to work from Monday to Friday. I _____ go to work on Saturday.

4. I buy fruit at Ray's Supermarket. I _____ buy fruit at Al's Supermarket.

5. Anna likes apples. She _____ like oranges.

6. Greg and Ivan run on Saturdays. They _____ run on Sundays.

7. I talk a lot. You _____ talk very much.

8. Mark and I eat at restaurants on the weekend. We _____ eat at home.

❹ Complete the sentences with the affirmative or negative form. Use the verbs in parentheses.

1. I _____*like*_____ wearing pants. They're good for work. I _____*don't like*_____ wearing dresses. (like)

2. Gina _____ in the morning. She likes to run before school.
She _____ in the evening. (run)

3. Ben's favorite store is BigMart. He _____ all his food at BigMart.
He _____ his food at FreshMart. (buy)

4. Rob and Carla are doctors. They _____ at Mercy Hospital.
They _____ at the school. (work)

5. You have a class at 6:30 P.M. You _____ the office at 5:30 P.M.
You _____ the office at 7:00 P.M. (leave)

6. Chen is from China. He _____ Chinese. He _____
Spanish. (speak)

Count and Noncount Nouns pages 76–77

Count and Noncount Nouns		
		Examples
Count Nouns	Count nouns are things we can count. They have a singular and plural form.	one apple / two apples one boy / three boys one peanut / four peanuts one grape / eight grapes
Noncount Nouns	Noncount nouns are things we cannot count. They are usually singular.	coffee bread water fish

1 Write the words in the correct column in the chart.

apples	butter	fish	oil	rice
bananas	carrots	grapes	onions	tomatoes
beans	cereal	lettuce	oranges	water
bread	chicken	milk	peanuts	yogurt

Count Nouns	Noncount Nouns

2 Circle the correct word or phrase.

1. I eat two **apple/apples** every day.

2. They sell **fish/fishes** at the market. They also sell **tomato/tomatoes**.

3. Maria likes **lettuce/lettuces**. She doesn't like **banana/bananas**.

4. I don't eat **bread/breads** for breakfast.

5. Brown **rice/rices** is healthy.

6. Josh drinks **coffee/coffees** and eats one **egg/eggs** for breakfast every day.

3 Write 3 sentences using count or noncount nouns.

1. I like _____ and _____.

2. I eat _____ and _____ for lunch.

3. I buy _____ and _____ at the supermarket.

Want and *Need*

Statements			Negative Statements			
I You	want	an ice cream cone.	I You	don't	want	healthy food.
He She	wants		He She	doesn't		
We They	want		We They	don't		
I You	need	water to live.	I You	don't	need	coffee to live.
He She	needs		He She	doesn't		
We They	need		We They	don't		

1 **Complete the sentences. Write the correct form of *want* or *need*. Use the affirmative or negative.**

1. Adam's new car is expensive. He _____ needs _____ a job.

2. Leah likes ice cream. She _____ some ice cream now.

3. I'm very sick. I _____ a doctor.

4. We _____ this box of cereal. It's too expensive.

5. You _____ chocolate to live. It's more important to eat vegetables.

6. We _____ a new TV. The old one is too small.

7. You _____ a driver's license to drive in the United States.

8. Ms. Cooper _____ a new job. She likes her job.

9. The students _____ pizza for lunch every day. They like pizza.

10. I _____ a truck. Trucks use a lot of gas. Gas is expensive.

2 **Complete the sentences about you.**

1. I want _____

2. I need _____

3. I don't want _____

4. I don't need _____

Simple Present, *Wh*-Questions

pages 80–81

Simple Present, *Wh*-Questions

Questions				Answers
What	do	I you	need?	A book.
Where	does	he she	live?	In New York.
When	do	we you they	leave?	At 1:00 P.M.

1 Check (✓) the correct answer.

1. What do you want for dinner?
○ Fish.　　　　　　　○ 6:00 P.M.

2. Where does your sister live?
○ A cup of coffee.　　○ In Omaha.

3. When does he go to work?
○ At 7:00 A.M.　　　　○ At the bank.

4. What do we need for school?
○ Books and pens.　　○ On Main St.

5. When does the party start?
○ At 5:00 P.M.　　　　○ Pizza and cake.

6. Where do you work?
○ At the library.　　　○ On Tuesdays.

2 Unscramble the questions. Then write your answers.

　　　　　　　　　　　　　　　　　　　　　　ANSWERS

1. do / live / Where / you / ?
　　Where do you live?　　　　　　　　_In Los Angeles._

2. eat / What / you / for breakfast / do?
　　_____　　　　_____

3. your class / start / When / does / ?
　　_____　　　　_____

4. leave class / When / you / do / ?
　　_____　　　　_____

5. your family / does / buy groceries / Where / ?
　　_____　　　　_____

6. bring to school / you / What / do /?
　　_____　　　　_____

LESSON 1 **Simple Present of *Have*** pages 88–89

Simple Present of *Have*

Statements			Negative Statements			
I You	have		I You	don't		
He She	has	a sister.	He She	doesn't	have	a brother.
We They	have		We They	don't		

1 Look at the photos. Complete the sentences with *have*, *has*, *don't have*, or *doesn't have*.

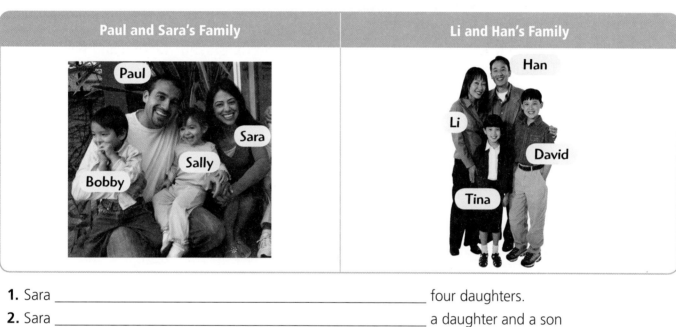

Paul and Sara's Family	Li and Han's Family

1. Sara _____ four daughters.

2. Sara _____ a daughter and a son

3. Han _____ two children.

4. Li and Han _____ two sons.

5. Han _____ a wife.

6. Sara and Li _____ husbands.

7. Sara and Han _____ grandchildren.

8. Sally _____ a sister.

2 Write sentences about you and your family.

1. I have _____

2. I don't have _____

3. My mother has _____

4. My mother doesn't have _____

Simple Present, *Yes / No* Questions

pages 90–91

Simple Present, *Yes / No* Questions

	Questions				Answers				
Do	I you			I you	do.		I you	don't.	
Does	he she	live here? work at night?	Yes,	he she	does.	No,	he she	doesn't.	
Do	we you they			we you they	do.		we you they	don't.	

---

1 Read the paragraph. Circle the verbs in the simple present.

Tatiana Ilyich is from Russia. Her grandparents still live in Russia, but Tatiana and her parents and brother live in New Jersey. Her father works at a bank. Her mother doesn't work. She goes to school and learns English. Tatiana and her brother go to school, too. Tatiana studies at a community college. Her brother Alex is in high school. Everyone in the family helps around the house. Her mother does the laundry and cooks meals. Her father goes grocery shopping and fixes things. Her brother washes the dishes. Tatiana makes the beds and takes out the trash. She doesn't like to take out the trash. In the evening, the children watch TV or do homework. Tatiana's parents don't watch TV. They like to read.

2 Complete the questions. Then answer the questions about Tatiana's family.

1. _____Does_____ Tatiana go to school? _____Yes, she does._____

2. _____ her grandparents live in New Jersey? _____

3. _____ Tatiana live in Russia? _____

4. _____ her father work at a hospital? _____

5. _____ Tatiana and her brother go to school? _____

6. _____ Alex go to a community college? _____

7. _____ Tatiana's parents cook meals together? _____

8. _____ Tatiana like to take out the trash? _____

9. _____ Tatiana and Alex read in the evening? _____

3 Write the words in the correct order to make questions. Then write answers.

1. you / live / Do / with / your parents / ?

_____

Your answer: _____

2. live / with you / your brother / Does / ?

_____

Your answer: _____

3. children / Do / have / you / ?

_____

Your answer: _____

4. you / clean / Do / the house / every week / ?

_____

Your answer: _____

5. brothers and sisters / your father / Does / have / ?

_____

Your answer: _____

4 Use the information to ask questions. Then complete the chart.

Find someone who...	Person's Name
pays the bills in his/her home.	1. _____
eats cereal for breakfast.	2. _____
has more than four brothers and sisters.	3. _____
lives with his/her grandparents.	4. _____
goes to the mall on weekends.	5. _____

I	always		cook.	✳	100% **always**
You	usually			✳	70–90% **usually**
He	often		washes the dishes.	✳	60% **often**
She				✳	
We	sometimes		eat breakfast.	✳	50% **sometimes**
They	never			✳	0% **never**

Adverbs of Frequency

1 Thien, Luan and Pou live together. Look at their schedule for the week. Then complete the sentences. Use adverbs of frequency.

Sunday	Monday	Tuesday	Wednesday	Thursday	Friday	Saturday
Thien – breakfast	Thien – breakfast	Thien – breakfast	Pou – breakfast	Thien – breakfast	Pou – breakfast	Pou – breakfast
Luan – dinner	Luan – dinner	Luan – dinner	Luan – dinner	Luan – dinner	Luan – dinner	Luan – dinner
Pou – dishes	Pou – dishes	Thien – dishes	Pou – dishes	Pou – dishes	Thien – dishes	Pou – dishes
Pou – walks the dog	Pou – walks the dog	Pou – walks the dog	Thien – walks the dog	Pou – walks the dog	Pou – walks the dog	Thien – walks the dog

1. Luan _____always_____ cooks dinner.

2. Pou _____ washes the dishes.

3. Thien _____ cooks breakfast.

4. Luan _____ walks the dog.

5. Pou _____ walks the dog.

6. Thien _____ washes the dishes.

2 Write about you. Complete the sentences with adverbs of frequency.

1. I _____ cook dinner.

2. My family and I _____ play cards.

3. I _____ play soccer with my friends on weekends.

4. My parents _____ tell stories about their childhoods.

5. We _____ listen to music in the car.

6. I _____ talk to my friends on the phone.

7. I _____ email my friends and family in my country.

8. I _____ read the newspaper in English.

❸ Match the questions and answers.

Questions

1. __c__ How often do you cook dinner?

2. _____ Who cleans the house?

3. _____ Do you play soccer every weekend?

4. _____ Do you always read the newspaper in the morning?

5. _____ Do you ever dance?

6. _____ How often do you listen to music in the evening?

Answers

a. No, I never dance.

b. Yes, we always play soccer on the weekends.

c. I never cook dinner.

d. No. I sometimes read it at night.

e. I usually listen to music in the evening.

f. I always clean the house.

❹ Answer the questions about you.

1. What do you eat for breakfast?

_____

2. How often do you go to a park on weekends?

_____

3. What do you do in the evenings?

_____

4. What do you eat for dinner?

_____

5. What do you and your friends do on the weekends?

_____

6. What do you do on your birthday?

_____

7. How often do you go to restaurants?

_____

8. Who pays the bills in your home?

_____

Compound Sentences with *and* and *but*

		Compound Sentences
Use *and* to connect two sentences with similar ideas.	I **play soccer** on the weekend. I **watch TV** on the weekend.	I play soccer on the weekend, **and** I watch TV on the weekend.
Use *but* to connect two sentences with different ideas.	He **plays soccer** on the weekend. He **doesn't play soccer** during the week.	He plays soccer on the weekend, **but** he doesn't play soccer during the week.

① Combine the sentences below with *and*.

1. We go to school in the morning. We work in the evening.

_____

2. Jack plays the guitar. He sings.

_____

3. Maria slices the vegetables. Her sister makes the salad.

_____

4. Brad lives alone. He does all the chores.

_____

5. Matt reads the newspaper. Then he watches TV.

_____

② Combine the sentences below with *but*.

1. Jenna loves Mark. Mark doesn't love her.

_____

2. My family lives in Mexico. I live here.

_____

3. I want to visit my country. I don't have money.

_____

4. My brother doesn't play an instrument. I play the piano.

_____

5. We usually go to the park on Sundays. Today it is raining.

_____

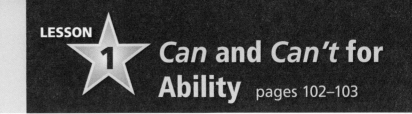

Can and *Can't* for Ability								
Statements				**Negative Statements**				
I You He She We You They	can	play use	basketball. a computer.	I You He She We You They	cannot can't	play use	basketball. a computer.

1 **Read the story. Complete the chart about Ana Maria.**

Ana Maria is seven years old. She can do many things. She can play baseball. She can dance. She can read and she can write. She wants a bicycle, but she can't ride a bicycle. She has a guitar, but she can't play the guitar. She can also help around the house. She can make her bed. She can take out the trash. She can wash the dishes. She likes food, but she can't cook. She has a dog, but she can't walk the dog. It is too big and strong!

Ana Maria can . . .	**Ana Maria can't . . .**
play baseball	

2 **Complete the sentences. Write *can* or *can't*.**

1. José's leg hurts. He _____can't_____ play soccer.

2. My toe hurts. I _____ wear shoes.

3. Our son is good at music. He _____ play the piano.

4. I know two languages. I _____ speak Spanish and English.

5. My teacher's throat hurts. She _____ speak in class.

6. Janice's fingers hurt. She _____ play the guitar today.

7. Our car is broken. We _____ drive it.

8. You don't have money. You _____ buy new shoes.

3 Complete the conversations. Use *can't* and the words in parentheses. Then practice with a partner.

1. A: What's wrong?

   B: My knee hurts. I _____*can't play soccer*_____. (play soccer)

2. A: What's the problem?

   B: Her ankle hurts. She _____. (walk)

3. A: What's the matter?

   B: His throat hurts. He _____. (talk)

4. A: Are you okay?

   B: My eyes hurt. I _____. (see)

5. A: What's the problem?

   B: His neck hurts. He _____. (drive)

6. A: What's wrong?

   B: My teeth hurt. I _____. (eat)

7. A: Are you okay?

   B: My head hurts. I _____. (sleep)

4 Write sentences about you. Use *can* or *can't* and the words in the box. Tell your partner.

cook	drive	ride a bicycle	play baseball
dance	fix things	speak English	play an instrument

1. _____ *I can speak English.* _____

2. _____

3. _____

4. _____

5. _____

6. _____

7. _____

8. _____

Questions with *Can* pages 104–105

Questions with *Can*

	Yes/No Questions				Answers					
Can	I you he she we they	speak play	Mandarin? the guitar?	Yes,	I you she he we they	can.	No,	I you he she we they	can't.

① Complete the conversations. Use the words in parentheses. Then practice with a partner.

1. A: _____Can you speak?_____ (speak / you)

   B: Yes, _____I can_____. My sore throat is better.

2. A: _____ (drive / she)

   B: No, _____. Her leg hurts.

3. A: _____ (go to the PTA meeting /he)

   B: Yes, _____. His backache is better.

4. A: _____ (dance / you)

   B: No, _____. My foot still hurts.

5. A: _____ (work tonight / they)

   B: No, _____. They have class.

6. A: _____ (go to school / I)

   B: No, _____. You have a fever.

② Write 4 questions. Use *can*. Then ask and answer the questions with a partner.

Example: _____Can you play the piano?_____

1. _____

2. _____

3. _____

4. _____

Should and *Shouldn't* for Advice

pages 106–107

Should and Shouldn't for Advice						
Statements				**Negative Statements**		
I You He She We They	should	**take** aspirin. **use** ear drops.		I You He She We They	should not shouldn't	**take** aspirin. **use** ear drops.

1 Read the information. Give advice. Complete the sentences with *should* or *shouldn't*.

Paulo is sick today. He has a fever and a cough. He also has a runny nose and a headache. What should he do?

1. He _____shouldn't_____ go to work today.

2. He _____ play soccer today.

3. He _____ take aspirin for his fever.

4. He _____ put heat on his ankle.

5. He _____ take cough medicine.

6. He _____ use ear drops.

7. He _____ rest.

8. He _____ drink liquids.

2 Read the sentences. Give advice. Use *should* or *shouldn't*.

1. Susana has a sore throat.

_____*She should eat soft food.*_____

2. Roger has a sprained ankle.

_____

3. Natasha has a headache.

_____

4. I have a backache.

_____

5. Louis and John have coughs.

_____

LESSON 4 — Object Pronouns pages 108–109

Object Pronouns

Subject Pronouns		Object Pronouns		Subject Pronoun		Object Pronoun	
I You	need help.	The doctor sees	me. you.				
He She	needs help.		him. her.	It They	is good. are good.	I am eating I am eating	it. them.
We They	need help.		us. them.				

1 **Write the object pronoun.**

1. <u>Luis</u> has the flu. Luis's friends take care of <u>him.</u>

2. <u>Josefina</u> has a sprained ankle. Her husband is carrying _____ into the hospital.

3. Chul takes two <u>tablets</u> for his backache. He takes _____ in the morning.

4. <u>I</u> have a fever. My husband is taking care of _____.

5. <u>The children</u> are very sick. The doctors are helping _____.

6. <u>My friend and I</u> have sore throats. The doctor is examining _____ right now.

7. She needs to take her <u>medicine</u> in the morning. She needs to take _____ with food.

8. <u>My brother</u>'s foot hurts. I am helping _____ to the waiting room.

2 **Rewrite the sentences. Replace the underlined words with object pronouns.**

1. He takes <u>the tablets</u> twice a day. _____ *He takes them twice a day.* _____

2. I can carry <u>John</u> into the hospital. _____

3. The doctors are examining <u>my sister</u> now. _____

4. I take <u>the medicine</u> in the morning. _____

5. Antonio drives <u>my sister and me</u> to school every day. _____

6. The doctor puts <u>the ear drops</u> in my ear. _____

7. We put a bandage on <u>Jack</u>. _____

8. You need to keep <u>your arm</u> dry. _____

Adjective Order

	Number	Size	Age	Color	Noun
It's an			old	brown	desk.
They are		big	new	yellow	chairs.
We have	two	medium-sized		green	sofas.
There are	three	large		blue	rugs.

1 **Unscramble the words to make sentences.**

1. a / lamp / white / small / it's   <u>It's a small white lamp.</u> .

2. wants / pink / large / sofa / a / she   _____ .

3. has / green / big / she / plants   _____ .

4. two / bathtubs / are / there / yellow   _____ .

5. green / refrigerator / a / big / it's   _____ .

6. blue / is / dresser / old / it / an   _____ .

2 **Write sentences about the picture. Use two adjectives in each sentence.**

1. <u>There is a small green plant.</u>
2. _____
3. _____
4. _____
5. _____
6. _____

3 **Answer the questions about your home. Use two adjectives in each sentence.**

1. What do you have in your kitchen? _____
2. What do you have in your living room? _____
3. What do you have in your bedroom? _____
4. What do you have in your bathroom? _____

LESSON 2

Simple Past of *Be* pages 118–119

Simple Past of *Be*, Statements

I	was	
You	were	
He / She / It	was	cold yesterday.
We / You / They	were	

1 Complete the sentences. Write *was* or *were*.

1. The front yard ___was___ big.
2. The kitchen _____ colorful.
3. The dressers _____ new.
4. She _____ happy.
5. I _____ tired.
6. The bathroom _____ small.
7. The bedrooms _____ blue.
8. Our old living room _____ big.
9. The trees _____ beautiful.
10. You _____ confused.

2 Write sentences. Use the past of *be* and the words in parentheses.

1. (garage / small) ___The garage was small.___
2. (bedrooms / blue) _____
3. (I / at the bank) _____
4. (John / a teacher) _____
5. (we / in class) _____
6. (the living room / sunny) _____
7. (the flowers / yellow) _____
8. (the yard / big) _____
9. (you / at home) _____
10. (closets / green) _____
11. (front door / red) _____
12. (my parents / happy) _____

TARGET GRAMMAR: UNIT 9 187

Simple Past of *Be*, Negative Statements

I	wasn't	
You	weren't	
He She It	wasn't	at work last night.
We You They	weren't	

3 Read the sentences. Write *was, wasn't, were* or *weren't*.

1. Our old house _____was_____ small.

2. The kitchen _____ blue. It was yellow.

3. The living room and dining room _____ brown. They weren't white.

4. My parents _____ sad. They were happy.

5. My father _____ in China in 2001. Now he is in the United States.

6. The living room _____ sunny. There were many windows.

7. My bedroom _____ small, but I _____ happy.

8. My sister and I _____ in one bedroom. We _____ best friends.

9. The closets _____ too small for me. I have a lot of clothes.

4 Write sentences about where you lived before. Use the past of *be*. Make some sentences negative.

Example: *The closets weren't big.*

1. _____

2. _____

3. _____

4. _____

5. _____

6. _____

Now tell a partner about your old home.

Simple Past of Regular Verbs pages 120–121

Simple Past of Regular Verbs

Statements			Negative Statements		
I You He She It We They	worked started	yesterday.	I You He She It We They	did not work didn't work didn't start	yesterday.

Spelling Rules	Examples
most regular verbs: add -**ed**	cook**ed**, email**ed**, play**ed**
verbs that end in e: add -**d**	lik**ed**, danc**ed**
verbs that end in consonant + *y*: change the –*y* to -**ied**	stud**ied**
verbs that end in consonant + 1 vowel + 1 consonant: double the last consonant, add -**ed**	trip**ped**, slip**ped**

1 **Complete the conversations. Use the past tense. Then practice with a partner.**

1. A: What happened to William?

   B: ___He slipped___ in the shower. (slip)

2. A: What happened to you?

   B: I'm tired. _____ home from work. (walk)

3. A: What's wrong with Christy and Josh?

   B: They're tired. _____ all evening. (dance)

4. A: What happened to Mathew?

   B: _____ his hand. (sprain)

5. A: What's wrong with your sister?

   B: She's tired. _____ in the garden all morning. (work)

6. A: What happened to you and Beth?

   B: _____ over a ladder in the garage. (trip)

7. A: What's wrong with George and Jeffrey?

   B: They're tired. _____ all night. (study)

2 Look at Rosalie's schedule from last weekend. Finish the sentences. Use the past tense of the verbs in parentheses. Some sentences are negative.

Rosalie's Schedule from Last Weekend	
Saturday	Sunday
9:00 Study	10:00 Work
1:00 Play basketball with Bob	4:00 Play the guitar with Sam
3:00 Email friends	5:00 Listen to music
7:00 Cook dinner with Tara	7:00 Walk the dog
9:00 Dance	9:00 Watch TV

1. Rosalie _____studied_____ on Saturday morning. (study)

2. Rosalie and Tara _____ at 7:00 on Saturday. (cook)

3. Rosalie _____ the dog on Saturday night. (walk)

4. Rosalie _____ on Sunday morning. (work)

5. Rosalie and Sam _____ the guitar at 4:00 on Sunday. (play)

6. Rosalie _____ friends at 7:00 on Sunday. (email)

7. Rosalie _____ TV on Sunday night. (watch)

8. Rosalie _____

9. Rosalie _____

10. Rosalie _____

3 Write about your schedule from last weekend. Use the past tense. Write 5 affirmative statements and 5 negative statements.

1. _____On Saturday morning, I cleaned the house._____

2. _____

3. _____

4. _____

5. _____

6. _____

7. _____

8. _____

9. _____

10. _____

Can, May, and *Would like* for Requests and Offers pages 122–123

Can and *May* for Requests and Offers

Requests				Offers			
Can	I	speak	to Lynn, please?	Can	I	help	you?
May	we	see	the apartment?	May	I	show	you the apartment?

Would like for Requests

I	would like	a small apartment.
We	would like	to see the condo.

1 **Match the questions and the answers. Then practice with a partner.**

1. ____e____ May I talk to Nancy?
2. _____ I would like two bedrooms.
3. _____ He would like to pay around $700.
4. _____ May I see the condo today?
5. _____ Can I look at the mobile home ad?
6. _____ Can we see the apartment tomorrow?
7. _____ I would like to live near my school.
8. _____ Can I call you tomorrow?

a. How about $750?
b. Sure. You can come see it tomorrow at 6:00.
c. Yes. My phone number is 555-0095.
d. Here's an ad for a two-bedroom apartment.
e. Sure, here she is.
f. Okay. There is a condo next to it.
g. Sorry, not today. How about tomorrow?
h. Sure, here it is.

2 **Write a request or offer for each situation. Use *may, can* or *would like*.**

1. You want to talk to Nancy.

_____

2. You want to see the backyard.

_____

3. You want to look at the ad for the mobile home.

_____

4. You want to drive your friend to school.

_____

5. You want to see the ad for the apartment.

_____

6. You want to help your friend look for a condo near your home.

_____

Simple Past of Irregular Verbs

Statements			Negative Statements			
I You He She We They	went	to school yesterday.	I You He She We They	didn't	go	to school yesterday.

Irregular Past Tense Verbs

present	past	present	past	present	past
come	came	go	went	see	saw
do	did	have	had	sleep	slept
eat	ate	make	made	spend	spent
get	got	put	put	take	took

1 Complete the sentences. Use the past tense of the verbs in parentheses.

1. They _____saw_____ (see) a movie last weekend.

2. I _____ (make / not) dinner last night.

3. He _____ (have) a great time at the party yesterday.

4. She _____ (go / not) to school yesterday.

5. They _____ (spend) the day at the shopping center.

6. John _____ (eat) Mexican food yesterday.

7. We _____ (get / not) a new car. This is our old one.

8. Sandy _____ (sleep) for ten hours.

9. I _____ (go) home early last night.

10. You _____ (take) the test last week.

2 Write five sentences about what you did yesterday. Use the past tense and the verbs in parentheses.

1. (eat) _____

2. (see) _____

3. (make) _____

4. (go) _____

5. (have) _____

Future with *Will* pages 132–133

Future with *Will*						
Statements				**Negative Statements**		
I You He She We You They	**will**	**go**	home tomorrow.	I You He She We You They	**will not won't**	**go** home tomorrow.

Contractions		
I will	=	I'll
you will	=	you'll
he will	=	he'll
she will	=	she'll
we will	=	we'll
you will	=	you'll
they will	=	they'll
will not	=	won't

❶ Complete the sentences. Use the future with *will*.

1. I have an interview tomorrow. I _____will get_____ (get) a haircut tonight.

2. Sue's first day of work is Wednesday. She _____ (get) there early.

3. Don't wait for me. I _____ (be) late tonight.

4. I need identification for the interview. I _____ (bring) my driver's license.

5. The job doesn't sound good. You _____ (get / not) benefits or paid vacation.

6. My sons don't have jobs. I don't know what they _____ (do) after school.

7. They _____ (call) people for interviews next week.

8. Don't worry. The test _____ (be / not) hard.

9. I called the plumber. He _____ (fix) the sink tomorrow.

10. My parents _____ (visit) us next month. I can't wait to see them!

❷ Write sentences about you. Use *will* or *won't*.

1. Tonight _____

2. Tomorrow _____

3. Next weekend _____

4. Next summer _____

5. Next year _____

Adverbs of Manner pages 134–135

Adverbs of Manner			
Adjectives	**Adverbs**	**Examples**	**Irregular Adverbs**
neat	neat**ly**	She dressed **neatly** for the interview.	good → **well** hard → **hard** fast → **fast**
quiet	quiet**ly**	I worked **quietly** at my desk.	
slow	slow**ly**	We read the résumé **slowly**.	
careful	careful**ly**	You should drive **carefully**.	

1 Complete the sentences with adverbs. Use the adjectives in parentheses.

1. Mary types _____quickly_____. (quick)

2. Bob reads the newspaper _____ every day. (careful)

3. Miguel dresses _____. (good)

4. Katrina speaks _____ on the phone. (quiet)

5. The boss speaks _____. (loud)

6. Ali and Robert work _____. (slow)

7. We dress _____ on Friday. (casual)

8. Tina works very _____ . (hard)

9. You shouldn't type so _____. You will make a mistake. (fast)

10. My interview was very good. I answered the questions _____. (good)

11. Carl painted the house _____. (careless)

2 Think of three important things you should do at a job interview. Use adverbs in your sentences. Compare your list with a partner. Discuss.

Example: <u>You should dress neatly for a job interview.</u>

1. _____

2. _____

3. _____

Future with *Be going to* pages 136–137

Future with *Be going to*

I	am			I	am not			
You	are			You	aren't			
He	is	going to	look for a new job.	He	isn't	going to	look for a new job.	
She				She				
We	are			We	aren't			
You				You				
They				They				

1 These people have goals for their lives. Complete the sentences about their lives. Use the correct form of *be going to*.

Name	Goal
Ping	continue English classes
Chuck and Jan	get a part-time job in a restaurant
Rodney	become a landscaper
Carol and Isabella	get driver's licenses
Kelly	become an office manager
Rico	open a hair salon

1. Rodney _____*is going to*_____ become a landscaper.

2. Chuck and Jan _____ get part-time jobs.

3. Kelly _____ continue English classes.

4. Rodney and Ping _____ open a hair salon.

5. Ping _____ continue English classes.

6. Carol and Isabella _____ get driver's licenses.

7. Kelly _____ become an office manager.

8. Jan _____ become a landscaper.

9. Carol _____ get a part-time job.

10. Rico _____ open a hair salon.

2 Now, write three goals for yourself. Tell them to a partner.

1. _____

2. _____

3. _____

Be going to, Yes / No Questions

Questions					Answers					
Am	I				I	am.		I	'm not	
Are	you				you	are.		you	aren't.	
Is	he she it	going to	come tomorrow?	Yes,	he she it	is.	No,	he she it	isn't.	
Are	we you they				we you they	are.		we you they	aren't.	

❸ Unscramble the questions. Then match the questions and the answers.

1. ___d___ get / a job / you / Are / to / going ?
   _____Are you going to get a job?_____

2. _____ going / Is / to / for a new job / he / look ?
   _____

3. _____ to / for jobs now / Are / going / they / look?
   _____

4. _____ going / a big job fair / Is / be/ to / it ?
   _____

5. _____ the job / take / to / going / Lisa / Is ?
   _____

6. _____ I / Am / see / to / going / you tomorrow ?
   _____

7. _____ we / to /Are / going / time to eat lunch / have?
   _____

8. _____ to / going / Are / apply / you and Tom/ for those jobs?
   _____

a. No, they aren't. They're going to go to college.

b. Yes, she is. She's very excited about it.

c. Yes, we are. They are going to take a break soon.

d. Yes, I am. I have an interview tomorrow.

e. Yes, it is. Many employers are going to be there.

f. No, he isn't. He likes his job now.

g. No, we aren't. They don't offer paid vacation.

h. No, you aren't. I can't come to the job fair.

❹ Answer the questions.

1. Are you going to look for a job soon? _____

2. Are you going to eat soon? _____

3. Are you going to go to bed soon? _____

ALL-STAR STUDENT BOOK 1 AUDIO SCRIPT

Note: This audio script offers support for many of the activities in the Student Book. When the words on the Student Book page are identical to those on the audio program, the script is not provided here.

UNIT ONE

Lesson 1: 2. Listen and Circle (page 4)
Listen to the conversation. Circle the correct name.

1.A: Hi. What's your name?
  B: My name is Tam.
  A: How do you spell that?
  B: T-a-m.
  A: Where are you from?
  B: I'm from Vietnam.

2.A: Hello. What's your name?
  B: My name's Amine.
  A: How do you spell that?
  B: A-m-i-n-e.
  A: Where are you from?
  B: Morocco.

3.A: Hi. What's your name?
  B: My name is Alex.
  A: How do you spell that?
  B: A-l-e-x.
  A: Where are you from?
  B: Russia.

Lesson 2: 1. Learn New Words (page 6)
Look at the picture. Listen to the words. Then listen and repeat.

1. teacher	Where's the teacher?
2. wall	What's on the wall?
3. clock	Where's the clock?
4. door	Where's the door?
5. board	Where's the board?
6. eraser	Where's the eraser?
7. map	Where's the map?
8. desk	Where's the desk?
9. table	Where's the table?
10. notebook	Where's the notebook
11. pen	Where's the pen?
12. pencil	Where's the pencil?
13. piece of paper	Where's the piece of paper?
14. book	Where's the book?
15. floor	What's on the floor?
16. chair	Where's the chair?
17. computer	Where's the computer?
18. student	Where's the student?
19. bookbag	Where's the bookbag?

Lesson 2: 3. Listen and Complete (page 6)
Listen. Complete the sentences. Listen again to check your answers.

1.A: Where's the computer?
  B: It's on the table.

2.A: Where's the clock?
  B: It's on the wall.

3.A: Where's the bookbag?
  B: It's on the floor.

4.A: Where's the book?
  B: It's on the desk.

5.A: Where's the pen?
  B: It's on the table.

Lesson 4: 1. Learn New Words (page 10)
Look at the form on page 11. Listen to the words. Then listen and repeat.

1. middle name	His middle name is Richard.
2. address	His address is 1640 East Flower Street.
3. street	His street is East Flower Street.
4. city	His city is Los Angeles.
5. state	His state is California.
6. zip code	His zip code is 91012.
7. telephone number	His telephone number is 555-5678.
8. area code	His area code is 310.
9. birthplace	His birthplace is Sacramento.
10. birthdate	His birthdate is November 12, 1982.
11. gender	His gender is male.
12. male	His gender is male.
13. female	He is not female.
14. marital status	His marital status is married.
15. single	He is not single.
16. married	He is married.
17. divorced	He is not divorced.
18. occupation	His occupation is teacher.

Lesson 5: 1. Practice Pronunciation: Long *I* and Long *E* (page 12)
C. Listen and circle the word you hear.

1. E	5. T
2. my	6. nice
3. hi	7. we
4. bye	8. write

Lesson 6: 1. Learn New Words (page 14)
Look at the pictures. Listen to the words. Then listen and repeat.

1. dentist	Joan Cho is a **dentist**.
2. bus driver	Lori Fisher is a **bus driver**.
3. pharmacist	Ken Parker is a **pharmacist**.
4. doctor	Jeff Lambert is a **doctor**.
5. salesclerk	Paula Cruz is a **salesclerk**.
6. machinist	Steven Morales is a **machinist**.
7. police officer	Meg Lewis is a **police officer**.
8. nurse	Leo Brunov is a **nurse**.
9. cashier	Amy Sherman is a **cashier**.

Lesson 7: 1. Listening Review (page 16)
Look at the pictures and listen. Choose the correct answer: A, B, or C. Use the Answer Sheet.

1. Open your book.
2. Her book is on the floor.

3. She's a teacher.
4. It's a clock.
5. Raise your hand.

Lesson 7: 2. Dictation (page 16)
Listen and write the sentences you hear.

1. What's your name?
2. Where are you from?
3. It's on the desk.
4. Close the window.
5. Hi, how are you?

UNIT TWO
Lesson 1: 1. Learn New Words (page 18)
Look at the pictures. Listen to the words. Then listen and repeat.

1. fire station	There's a fire station on High Street.
2. police station	There's a police station on Pine Street.
3. post office	There's a post office on Main Street.
4. community center	There's a community center on Daniel Street.
5. library	There's a library on Low Street.
6. playground	There's a playground on Meadow Street.
7. school	There's a school on State Street.
8. park	There's a park on Meadow Street.
9. bank	There's a bank on Main Street.
10. drugstore	There's a drugstore on Pine Street.
11. gas station	There's a gas station on Green Street.
12. supermarket	There's a supermarket on North Street.
13. hospital	There's a hospital on Main Street.
14. laundromat	There's a laundromat on Daniel Street.
15. movie theater	There's a movie theater on Low Street.
16. restaurant	There's a restaurant on High Street.

Lesson 1: 2. Listen and Write (page 18)
Listen and write the telephone number next to each place.

1.A: There's a hospital on Main Street.
   B: What's the phone number?
   A: It's 643-555-1884.

2.A: There's a drugstore on Pine Street.
   B: What's the telephone number?
   A: 643-555-8823.

3.A: There's a restaurant on High Street.
   B: What's the phone number?
   A: 643-555-9164.

4.A: There's a laundromat on Daniel Street.
   B: What's the telephone number?
   A: 643-555-0254.

5.A: There's a police station on Pine Street.
   B: What's the phone number?
   A: 643-555-7190.

6.A: There's a supermarket on North Street.
   B: What's the telephone number?
   A: 643-555-3156.

Lesson 2: 1. Learn New Words (page 20)
Look at the pictures. Listen to the words. Then listen and repeat.

1. next to	The post office is next to the drugstore.
2. between	The laundromat is between the drugstore and the supermarket.
3. across from	The bank is across from the post office.
4. in front of	The playground is in front of the school.
5. in back of	There's a park in back of the library.
6. on the corner of	There's a gas station on the corner of State Street and Main Street.

Lesson 2: 3 Listen and Circle (page 20)
Look at the map on page 21. Listen to the questions and circle yes or no.

1. Is the drugstore between the post office and the laundromat?
2. Is the police station next to the school?
3. Is the fire station across from the supermarket?
4. Is the school in back of the park?
5. Is the restaurant between the drugstore and the supermarket?
6. Is the bank on the corner of State Street and Main Street?

Lesson 3: 2. Learn New Words (page 22)
Look at the picture. Listen to the words. Then listen and repeat.

1. parking lot	There's a parking lot next to the supermarket.
2. crosswalk	There's a crosswalk near the community center.
3. bus stop	There's a bus stop near the movie theater.
4. bus	There's a bus near the bus stop.
5. ambulance	There's an ambulance in front of the hospital.
6. sidewalk	There's a sidewalk in front of the movie theater.
7. truck	There's a truck on Pine Street.
8. stoplight	There's a stoplight on Main Street.
9. mailbox	There's a mailbox in front of the post office.
10. ATM	There's an ATM in front of the bank.
11. pay phone	There's a pay phone near Pine Street and Main Street.
12. taxi	There's a taxi across from the community center.
13. car	There's a car in front of the taxi.
14. vending machine	There's a vending machine in front of the community center.
15. stop	There's a stop sign on the corner of Meadow and Main Streets.
16. no parking	The sign says, "No parking."
17. do not enter	The sign says, "Do not enter."
18. no right turn	The sign says, "No right turn."
19. no left turn	The sign says, "No left turn."
20. one way	The sign says, "One way" only.

Lesson 4: 2. Learn New Words (page 24)
Look at the picture. Listen to the words. Then listen and repeat.

1. capital   The capital of New York is Albany.
2. north   Oklahoma is north of Texas.
3. south   California is south of Oregon.
4. east   North Carolina is east of Tennessee.
5. west   Illinois is west of Indiana.

Lesson 5: 1. Practice Pronunciation: Intonation (page 26)
B. Listen to the sentences. Check the correct use of Excuse me.

1. Excuse me? Can you repeat that, please?
2. Excuse me. Is there a mailbox near here?
3. Excuse me. Where's the library?
4. Excuse me?
5. Excuse me.

Lesson 6: 1. Learn New Words (page 28)
Look at the pictures. Listen to the words. Then listen and repeat.

1. librarian   The librarian checks out your books.
2. checkout desk   Bring your books to the checkout desk.
3. library card   Complete this application for a library card.
4. magazines   You can take out magazines.
5. audio CDs   You can take out audio CDs.
6. video DVDs   You can take out video DVDs.
7. children's books You can take out children's books.

Lesson 7: 1. Listening Review (page 30)
You will hear a question. Listen to the conversation. You will hear the question again. Choose the correct answer: A, B, or C. Use the Answer Sheet.

1. Where's the bus stop?
   A: Is there a bus stop near here?
   B: Yes. There's one on Main Street.

Where's the bus stop?
A. on Pine Street   B. on Main Street   C. on Front Street

2. Where's an ATM?
   A: Excuse me. Where's an ATM?
   B: It's next to the supermarket.

Where's the ATM?
A. next to the bank   B. next to the restaurant
C. next to the supermarket

3. Where's the restaurant?
   A: Is the restaurant on Green Street?
   B: No, it's on Pine Street.

Where's the restaurant?
A. on Pine Street   B. on Green Street   C. on Main Street

4. Is there a bank near the post office?
   A: Excuse me. Is there a bank near here?
   B: Yes, there's one across from the post office.

Is there a bank near the post office?
A. No, there isn't.   B. Yes, there is.   C. I don't know.

5. What's the problem?
   A: Is there a drugstore near here?
   B: I'm sorry. I don't speak English very well.

What's the problem?
A. She doesn't know.   B. She doesn't understand.
C. She's new in town.

Lesson 7: 2. Dictation (page 30)
Listen and write the words you hear.

1. A: Excuse me. Where's the supermarket?
   B: It's on Pine Street.

2. A: Excuse me. Is there a mailbox near here?
   B: Yes, there is. It's in front of the library.

3. A: What's the capital of New Mexico?
   B: I'm not sure.

4. A: Excuse me. Is there a pay phone around here?
   B: I'm sorry. I don't know.

5. A: What states are south of Canada?
   B: I'm not sure.

UNIT THREE

Lesson 1: 2. Learn New Words (page 32)
Look at the pictures. Listen to the words. Then listen and repeat.

1. 1:00   It's one o'clock.
2. 3:15   It's three-fifteen. It's quarter after three.
3. 5:30   It's five-thirty.
4. 7:45   It's seven-forty-five. It's quarter to eight.
5. It's noon. (12:00 P.M.)
6. It's midnight. (12:00 A.M.)
7. It's 9:00 A.M.
8. It's 9:00 P.M.
9. It's eight o'clock in the morning.
10. It's two-fifteen in the afternoon.
11. It's seven-thirty in the evening.
12. It's eleven forty-five at night.

Lesson 1: 4. Listen and Write (page 32)
Listen and write the times.

1. A: Excuse me. What time is it?
   B: It's 4:30.

2. A: Look at the time. It's already 3:15.
   B: Oh no! We're late for class.

3. A: Excuse me. Do you have the time?
   B: Sure. It's 7:45.

4. A: It's noon. We can go to lunch now.
   B: Good. I'm hungry.

5.A: Hey, Mom. What time is it?
  B: It's 5:00. Time to start doing your homework.

6.A: You look tired.
  B: I am tired. It's midnight.

Lesson 2: 1. Learn New Words (page 34)
Look at the picture. Listen to the words. Then listen and repeat.

1. open	The Children's Room is open.
2. closed	The Children's Room is not closed.
3. Sunday	The library is open on Sunday.
4. Monday	The library is closed on Monday.
5. Tuesday	The library is open on Tuesday.
6. Wednesday	The library is open on Wednesday.
7. Thursday	The library is closed on Thursday.
8. Friday	The library is open on Friday.
9. Saturday	The library is open on Saturday.
10. No smoking	There is no smoking in the library.
11. No eating	There is no eating in the library.
12. No cell phones	No cell phones in the library.

Lesson 2: 4. Listen and Circle (page 34)
Listen. Look at the picture. Circle the correct answer.

1. Is the library open today?
2. Are there windows in the library?
3. Are there seven children in the Children's Room?
4. Is there a computer on the checkout desk?
5. Is there a pay phone behind the checkout desk?
6. Is the time 10:35 a.m.?

Lesson 3: 1. Learn New Words (page 36)
Look at the pictures. Listen to the words. Then listen and repeat.

Coins
1. a penny
   one cent

2. a nickel
   five cents

3. a dime
   ten cents

4. a quarter
   twenty-five cents

5. a one-dollar coin
   one dollar

Bills
6. a one-dollar bill
   a dollar

7. a five-dollar bill
   five dollars

8. a ten-dollar bill
   ten dollars

9. a twenty-dollar bill
   twenty dollars

10. a fifty-dollar bill
    fifty dollars

11. a one hundred-dollar bill
    one hundred dollars

12. one thousand dollars

Lesson 4: 1. Learn New Words (page 38)
Look at the checks. Listen to the words. Then listen and repeat.

1. check	It's a check.
2. check number	The check number is one twenty-four.
3. amount	The check amount is twelve dollars and seventy-five cents.
4. signature	It's David's signature.
5. memo	The memo line reads "for food."
6. account number	The account number is 123-456-7.

Lesson 5: 1. Practice Pronunciation: Thirteen or Thirty? (page 40)
B. Listen and circle the numbers you hear.

1. 13	5. 17
2. 40	6. 80
3. 50	7. 90
4. 16	

C. Listen and circle the numbers you hear.

1. It's six-fifteen.
2. It's fifty cents.
3. From 9:30 a.m. to 6:00 p.m.
4. The price is $3.18.

Lesson 5: 4. Listen and Write (page 41)

Thank you for calling the Lucas Library. For library hours, press 1. The library is open Monday through Thursday from 11:00 to 9:00. On Friday and Saturday, the library is open from 9:30 to 6:15. It's closed on Sunday. For information about our annual book sale, press 5. Come to our book sale on March 30 from 8:15 to 5:30. There are great prices on used books.

Lesson 6: 4. Listen and Write (page 43)
Listen and fill in the missing information on the paystub.

1. Stacy Ming earns $10.15 an hour.
2. Stacy's federal tax for this week is $60.90.
3. Stacy's state tax for this week is $36.54.
4. Stacy's total deductions are $97.44.
5. Stacy's net pay this week is $308.56.

Lesson 7: 1. Listening Review (page 44)
Listen to the conversation. To finish the conversation, listen and choose the correct answer: A, B, or C. Use the Answer Sheet.

1.
 A: Are you open on Friday?
 B: Yes, we are.
 A: What are your hours?

A. It's 9:00 A.M.
B. We're open from 9:00 A.M. to 7:00 P.M.
C. We close at 7:30 on Fridays.

2.
A: How can I help you?
B: How much is the table?

A. It's 50 dollars and 19 cents.
B. It's 9:15.
C. We open at 9:00.

3.
A: Oh no! I'm late!
B: What time is your appointment?

A. It's closed on Monday.
B. It's four dollars.
C. It's at 4:00.

4.
A: Hello. Westville Drugstore. Can I help you?
B: Yes. What are your hours on Sunday?

A. It's $6.50.
B. We're not open then.
C. Yes, it is.

5.
A: How much is it?
B: Seventy-five cents.

A. Okay. Here are three quarters.
B. Okay. Here are two quarters.
C. Yes, it is.

Lesson 7: 2. Dictation (page 44)
Listen and write the sentences you hear.
1. It's 4:30 in the morning.
2. It's 6:15 in the evening.
3. How much is it?
4. It's $17.30. (It's seventeen dollars and thirty cents)
5. Is the library open on Friday?

UNIT FOUR
Lesson 1:1. Learn New Words (page 46)
Look at the pictures. Listen to the words. Then listen and repeat.

1. January	It's January.
2. February	It's February.
3. March	It's March.
4. April	It's April.
5. May	It's May.
6. June	It's June.
7. July	It's July.
8. August	It's August.
9. September	It's September.
10. October	It's October.

11. November	It's November.
12. December	It's December.
13. hot	It's hot here.
14. warm	It's warm here.
15. sunny	It's sunny here.
16. snowy	It's snowy here.
17. cold	It's cold here.
18. cool	It's cool here.
19. cloudy	It's cloudy here.
20. rainy	It's rainy here.
21. windy	It's windy here.

Lesson 1: 4. Listen and Circle (page 46)
Listen to the conversations. Circle the correct word.
1. A: When is your birthday?
   B: It's in January.

2. A: When is your sister's birthday?
   B: Her birthday is in March.

3. A: What's your favorite month?
   B: I like October. It's cool.

4. A: How's the weather today?
   B: It's cloudy.

5. A: How's the weather in May?
   B: It's sunny here in May.

6. A: How's the weather in January?
   B: It's cold here in January.

Lesson 2: 1. Learn Ordinal Numbers (page 48)
Listen to the numbers. Then listen and repeat.

1. first	The first of May is on Tuesday.
2. second	The second of May is on Wednesday.
3. third	The third of May is on Thursday.
4. fourth	The fourth of May is on Friday.
5. fifth	The fifth of May is on Saturday.
6. sixth	The sixth of May is on Sunday.
7. seventh	The seventh of May is on Monday.
8. eighth	The eighth of May is on Tuesday.
9. ninth	The ninth of May is on Wednesday.
10. tenth	The tenth of May is on Thursday.
11. eleventh	The eleventh of May is on Friday.
12. twelfth	The twelfth of May is on Saturday.
13. thirteenth	The thirteenth of May is on Sunday.
14. fourteenth	The fourteenth of May is on Monday.
15. fifteenth	The fifteenth of May is on Tuesday.
16. sixteenth	The sixteenth of May is on Wednesday.

Lesson 2: 2. Learn New Words (page 48)
Look at the pictures. Listen to the words. Then listen and repeat.

1. doctor's appointment	Her doctor's appointment is on May first.
2. haircut appointment	Her haircut appointment is on May second.

3. computer class	Her computer class is on May third.
4. birthday party	Her birthday party is on May sixth.
5. PTA meeting	Her PTA meeting is on May eighth.
6. job interview	Her job interview is on May ninth.
7. basketball game	Her basketball game is on May eleventh.
8. dental appointment	Her dental appointment is on May fifteenth.

Lesson 2: 3. Listen and Circle (page 48)
Listen to the conversations. Look at the pictures. Circle True or False.

1. A: Is Alice's haircut on Thursday, May third?
   B: No, I think it's on Wednesday, May second.

2. A: When is Alice's basketball game?
   B: I think it's on the twelfth.

3. A: Is Alice's job interview on May tenth?
   B: Yes, it is.

4. A: When is Alice's birthday party?
   B: It's on Sunday.

5. A: Alice has a computer class on May third, right?
   B: Yes. At 7:00.

6. A: When is the PTA meeting?
   B: On Tuesday, May tenth.

Lesson 3: 1. Learn Ordinal Numbers
(page 50)
Listen to the numbers. Then listen and repeat.

1. seventeenth	The seventeenth of June is on Sunday.
2. eighteenth	The eighteenth of June is on Monday.
3. nineteenth	The nineteenth of June is on Tuesday.
4. twentieth	The twentieth of June is on Wednesday.
5. twenty-first	The twenty-first of June is on Thursday.
6. twenty-second	The twenty-second of June is on Friday.
7. twenty-third	The twenty-third of June is on Saturday.
8. twenty-fourth	The twenty-fourth of June is on Sunday.
9. twenty-fifth	The twenty-fifth of June is on Monday.
10. twenty-sixth	The twenty-sixth of June is on Tuesday.
11. twenty-seventh	The twenty-seventh of June is on Wednesday.
12. twenty-eighth	The twenty-eighth of June is on Thursday.
13. twenty-ninth	The twenty-ninth of June is on Friday.
14. thirtieth	The thirtieth of June is on Saturday.
15. thirty-first	There is no thirty-first of June.

Lesson 4: 4. Listen and Circle (page 52)
Listen to the conversations. Then circle the correct answers.

1.
   A: What's your favorite holiday?
   B: Independence Day.
   A: When is that?
   B: July 4th.

2.
   A: What's your favorite holiday?
   B: Memorial Day.
   A: When is that?
   B: It's in May.

3.
   A: When is the first day of school?
   B: It's Tuesday after Labor Day.
   A: When is Labor Day?
   B: It's the first Monday in September.

4.
   A: What's your favorite holiday in February?
   B: I like Valentine's Day.
   A: When is that?
   B: It's on February 14th.

5.
   A: Is Election Day in November?
   B: Yes, it is.
   A: What day is it on?
   B: It's on the first Tuesday after the first Monday in November.

Lesson 7: 1. Listening Review (page 58)
Look at the pictures and listen. Choose the correct answer: A, B, or C. Use the Answer Sheet.

1. A: How's the weather in May?
   B: It's warm here in May.

2. A: How's the weather in February?
   B: It's snowy here in February.

3. A: How's the weather today?
   B: It's cloudy today.

4. A: How's the weather in December?
   B: It's windy here in December.

5. A: How's the weather in August?
   B: It's hot in August.

Lesson 7: 2. Dictation (page 58)
Listen and write the sentences you hear.

1. It's rainy here in April.
2. When is your dental appointment?
3. Alice's basketball game is on May 11th.
4. My computer class is on Wednesday, June 3rd.
5. My birthday is on January 21st.

UNIT FIVE

Lesson 1: 1. Learn New Words (page 60)
Look at the pictures. Listen to the words. Then listen and repeat.

Clothes for Men

1. necktie	What is it? It's a necktie.
2. undershirt	What is it? It's an undershirt.
3. briefs	What are they? They're briefs.

Clothes for Men and Women

4. T-shirt	What is it? It's a T-shirt.
5. shirt	What is it? It's a shirt.
6. sweater	What is it? It's a sweater.
7. coat	What is it? It's a coat.
8. jacket	What is it? It's a jacket.
9. hat	What is it? It's a hat.
10. pants	What are they? They're pants.
11. shorts	What are they? They're shorts.
12. socks	What are they? They're socks.
13. shoes	What are they? They're shoes.
14. boots	What are they? They're boots.

Clothes for Women

15. skirt	What is it? It's a skirt.
16. dress	What is it? It's a dress.

Colors

17. blue	What color is it? Blue.
18. yellow	What color is it? Yellow.
19. red	What color is it? Red.
20. black	What color is it? Black.
21. brown	What color is it? Brown.
22. green	What color is it? Green.
23. purple	What color is it? Purple.
24. white	What color is it? White.

Lesson 1: 4. Listen and Match (page 60)
Listen and match the names and the pictures.

1. Sylvia's dress is green.
2. Tricia's shorts are blue.
3. Nick's jacket is brown.
4. Mark's shirt is purple.
5. Amanda's hat is blue and white.

Lesson 2: 1. Learn New Words (page 62)
Look at the picture. Listen to the words. Then listen and repeat.

People

1. cashier	The cashier is near the entrance.
2. customer	A customer is looking in the mirror.
3. fitting room attendant	The fitting room attendant is helping a customer.

Places

4. department store	This is Lane's Department Store.
5. customer service	There is a woman working at customer service.
6. exit	The exit is across from customer service.
7. entrance	There are people coming in the entrance.
8. fitting room	The fitting room is in the back of the store.

Actions

9. coming into (the store)	The man is coming into the store.
10. going into (the elevator)	The woman is going into the elevator.
11. sleeping	The boy is sleeping near the fitting room.
12. leaving	Marc and Tom are leaving the store.
13. running	A cashier is running after Tom.
14. buying (sweaters)	The woman is buying a lot of sweaters.
15. talking	The men are talking near the store directory.
16. trying on (a sweater)	Tim is trying on a sweater.
17. helping (a customer)	The salesclerk is helping a customer.

Lesson 2: 4. Listen and Circle (page 62)
Listen to the conversations. Look at the picture. Circle True or False.

1.
A: Hi, May. What's Tim doing?
B: He's buying a sweater.

2.
A: What's Jill doing?
B: She's returning sweaters.

3.
A: Is Karen in the store?
B: Yes, she is.
A: What's she doing?
B: She's trying on a hat.

4.
A: Where's Anna?
B: She's at customer service.
A: What's she doing?
B: She's returning pants.

5.
A: Where's Don?
B: He's near the store directory.
A: What's he doing?
B: He's talking to Ed.

Lesson 3: 1. Learn New Words (page 64)
Look at the pictures. Listen to the words. Then listen and repeat.

1. price tag	Where's the price tag?
2. size	What size is it?
3. S (small)	What size is it? This is a small.
4. M (medium)	What size is it? That's a medium.
5. L (large)	What size is it? It's a large.
6. XL (extra large)	What size is it? It's an extra large.
7. receipt	Where's the receipt?

Lesson 4: 4. Predict (page 66)
What is the missing word at the end of the story? Share ideas with your classmates.
SIMON: Here you are, Leo. Your old vest is now a necktie.

Lesson 5: 2. Learn New Words (page 68)
Look at the pictures. Listen to the words. Then listen and repeat.

1. long — The red skirt is long.
2. too long — The black skirt is too long.
3. short — The green skirt is short.
4. too short — The purple skirt is too short.
5. tight — The brown pants are tight.
6. too tight — The blue pants are too tight.
7. loose — The black pants are loose.
8. too loose — The green pants are too loose.

Lesson 7: 1. Listening Review (page 72)
You will hear a question. Listen to the conversation. You will hear the question again. Choose the correct answer: A, B, or C. Use your Answer Sheet.

1. What is John wearing?
   A: I like your necktie, John.
   B: Thank you. Blue is my favorite color.

What is John wearing?
   A. a blue sweater
   B. a blue shirt
   C. a blue necktie

2. What is Kate doing?
   A: Where's Kate?
   B: She's in the fitting room. She's trying on a dress.

What is Kate doing?
   A. She's buying a dress.
   B. She's trying on a dress.
   C. She's going into the fitting room.

3. How much are the shoes?
   A: Are these shoes on sale?
   B: Yes, they are. They're only $25.

How much are the shoes?
   A. $25.
   B. $20.
   C. On sale.

4. What's the problem?
   A: I'd like to return this dress.
   B: What's the problem?
   A. It's too short.
   B: All right.

What's the problem?
   A. The dress is too long.
   B. The dress is too short.
   C. The dress is too loose.

5. What is Mike trying on?
   A: Do you like these pants?
   B: They're nice, Mike, but I think they're too tight.

What is Mike trying on?
   A. a pair of pants
   B. a pair of shoes
   C. a tight jacket

Lesson 7: 2. Dictation (page 72)
Listen and write the sentences you hear.

1. What are you doing?
2. What are you wearing?
3. I'm trying on a sweater.
4. Joe is wearing brown pants and a white shirt.
5. I think that skirt is too short.

UNIT SIX

Lesson 1: 1. Learn New Words (page 74)
Look at the pictures. Listen to the words. Then listen and repeat. Add another food to each group.

1. noodles — I like noodles.
2. bread — He likes bread.
3. rice — She likes rice.
4. cereal — We like cereal.
5. apples — They like apples.
6. oranges — I like oranges.
7. grapes — He likes grapes.
8. bananas — She likes bananas.
9. milk — We like milk.
10. cheese — They like cheese.
11. yogurt — I like yogurt.
12. ice cream — He likes ice cream.
13. peanuts — She likes peanuts.
14. chicken — We like chicken.
15. fish — They like fish.
16. beans — I like beans.
17. onions — He likes onions.
18. tomatoes — She likes tomatoes.
19. lettuce — We like lettuce.
20. carrots — They like carrots.
21. butter — I like butter.
22. oil — He likes oil.
23. sugar — She likes sugar.

Lesson 1: 3. Listen and Check (page 74)
Listen. Check the foods you hear.

A: I'm going to the farmers' market.
B: What is a farmers' market?
A: People sell fresh food like fruit and vegetables.
B: Do they sell tomatoes?
A: Oh, yes, and lettuce, carrots, apples, and a lot of other food.
B: Do they only sell fruit and vegetables?
A: No, they also sell cheese and bread, and sometimes fish.

Lesson 2: 1. Learn New Words (page 76)
Look at the pictures. Listen to the words. Then listen and repeat.

1. aisle	Where is Aisle 1?
2. meat counter	Where's the meat counter?
3. checkout counter	Where's the checkout counter?
4. bakery	Where's the bakery?
5. produce section	Where's the produce section?
6. manager	Where's the manager?
7. bag	Where's the bag?
8. cart	Where is a cart?
9. basket	Where is a basket?
10. coupons	Where are the coupons?
11. push a cart	Who is pushing the cart?
12. look at	Who is looking at the bread?
13. eat	Who is eating something?
14. check out	Who is checking out?
15. stand in line	Who is standing in line?

Lesson 3: 1. Learn New Words (page 78)
Look at the picture. Listen to the words. Then listen and repeat.

1. a bag of apples	How much is a bag of apples?
2. a head of lettuce	How much is a head of lettuce?
3. a carton of milk	How much is a carton of milk?
4. a loaf of bread	How much is a loaf of bread?
5. a package of cheese	How much is a package of cheese?
6. a jar of honey	How much is a jar of honey?
7. a box of sugar	How much is a box of sugar?
8. a pound of chicken	How much is a pound of chicken?
9. a can of tomatoes	How much is a can of tomatoes?
10. a bottle of oil	How much is a bottle of oil?
11. expensive	That's expensive.
12. cheap	That's cheap.

Lesson 4: 3. Listen and Circle (page 80)
Listen to the conversations and circle your answers.

1. A: Where is orange juice 2 for $4, at Ray's Supermarket or Ford's?
   B: At Ray's.

2. A: How much does chicken cost at Ford's?
   B: It's $.99 a pound.

3. A: How many ounces of oil do you get for $2.99 at Ford's?
   B: Only 16 ounces. That's not a very big bottle.

4. A: How many pounds of carrots do you get for $6 at Ray's?
   B: Ten pounds. That's a lot of carrots.

5. A: How much does a bottle of oil cost at Ray's?
   B: It's $3.99 a bottle, but you get 96 ounces.

Lesson 5: . Practice Pronunciation: Intonation in *Yes/No* Questions (page 82)
B. Listen to the sentences. Then listen and repeat.

1. a. The apples are on sale.   2. a. Okay?   3. a. Milk.
   b. The apples are on sale?   b. Okay.   b. Milk?

4. a. Aisle 3.   5. a. Anything else?   6. a. The produce section?
   b. Aisle 3?   b. Nothing else.   b. The produce section.

Lesson 6: 1 Learn New Words (page 84)
Look at the menu. Listen to the words. Then listen and repeat.

Appetizers
Chicken soup	Chicken soup is $3.95
Green salad	A green salad is $4.50.
Onion rings	Onion rings are $5.95.
Fruit salad	A fruit salad is $4.50.

Side Dishes
Baked potato	A baked potato is $2.95.
Green beans	Green beans are $2.00.
Corn	Corn is $2.00.

Macaroni and cheese Macaroni and cheese is $2.50.

Main Courses
Hamburger	A hamburger is $6.95.
Fish sandwich	A fish sandwich is $7.95.
Pizza slice	A pizza slice is $2.50.
Half a chicken	A half a chicken is $8.95.

Beverages
Coffee	A cup of coffee is $1.50.
Tea	A cup of tea is $1.00.
Milk	A glass of milk is $2.00.
Soda	A glass of soda is $1.50.

For a platter, main dish with one side dish and beverage, add $2.00.

Lesson 6: 2. Listen and Write (pages 84–85)
Listen to the orders. Write what you hear.

A: What would you like today?
B: A hamburger and fruit salad, please.
A: Anything to drink?
B: Yes. Some milk, please.
A: And for you, sir?
C: I'd like the half chicken, please.
A: Do you want a platter?
C: What's the platter?
A: You get one side dish and a beverage for just $2 more.
C: Yes, I'll have a platter, with green beans and a coffee, please.
A: Thanks.

Lesson 7: 1. Listening Review (page 86)
Look at the pictures and listen. Choose the correct answer: A, B, or C. Use the Answer Sheet.

1. A: I'm buying some tomatoes.
   B: Great! They're on sale this week.

2. A: I like bananas.
   B: I don't.

3. A: Can I help you?
   B: Two pounds of chicken, please.

4.A: Where's Maria?
  B: She's standing in line.
5.A: Can I help you?
  B: I need a jar of honey.

Lesson 7: 2. Dictation (page 86)
Listen and write the sentences you hear.

  1. Bananas are in the produce section.
  2. Do you like rice?
  3. We need fish and chicken.
  4. Ann is checking out.
  5. A pound of cheese, please.

UNIT SEVEN
Lesson 1: 1. Learn New Words (page 88)
Look at the pictures of this family. Listen to the words.
Then listen and repeat.

  1. husband, Jack is Mei's husband.
  2. wife, Mei is Jack's wife.
  3. parents, Jack and Mei are parents. They are Ann's and Tim's parents.
  4. children, Ann and Tim are children. They are Jack and Mei's children.
  5. daughter, Ann is Mei's daughter.
  6. mother, Mei is Ann's mother.
  7. son, Tim is Jack's son.
  8. father, Jack is Tim's father.
  9. sister, Ann is Tim's sister.
  10. brother, Tim is Ann's brother.
  11. grandmother, Carol is Tim's grandmother.
  12. grandson, Tim is Carol's grandson.
  13. grandfather, Bob is Ann's grandfather.
  14. granddaughter, Ann is Bob's granddaughter.
  15. uncle, Jack is Kevin's uncle.
  16. nephew, Kevin is Jack's nephew.
  17. aunt, Jill is Ann's aunt.
  18. niece, Ann is Jill's niece.
  19. cousins, Ann and Kevin are cousins.

Lesson 1: 3. Listen and Match (page 88)
Listen to the interview. Match the names to the relatives.

A: Hello. What's your name?
B: Gina Porter.
A: Are you married, Gina?
B: Yes.
A: What's your husband's name?
B: Mark.
A: Do you have children?
B: Yes, I have one son and one daughter. My son's name is Brad. My daughter's name is Hannah.
A: Does anyone else live with you?
B: Yes, my sister and her daughter.

A: What are their names?
B: My sister's name is Linda Green. My niece's name is Karen Green.

Lesson 2:1. Learn New Words (page 90)
Look at the pictures. Listen to the words. Then listen and repeat.

1. fix things	Do you fix things at home?
2. make the bed	Do you make the bed at home?
3. wash the dishes	Do you wash the dishes at home?
4. take out the trash	Do you take out the trash at home?
5. go grocery shopping	Do you go grocery shopping?
6. pay the bills	Do you pay the bills at home?
7. clean the house	Do you clean the house?
8. do the laundry	Do you do the laundry?
9. cook dinner	Do you cook dinner?
10. feed the pets	Do you feed the pets?

Lesson 2: 2. Listen and Match (page 90)
Listen to the conversation. Match the name to the responsibility.

A: Hi Mei. How are you?
B: I'm fine, but I'm busy. Jack's parents are coming tomorrow. They visit every Sunday.
A: Do you have a lot to do?
B: Oh yes. We do a lot of chores before they visit. Jack does the laundry, and Ann takes out the trash. Tim makes his bed. We all go shopping for groceries, and I cook the dinner. We love their visits. And we have a clean house!

Lesson 3:1. Learn New Words (page 92)
Look at the picture. Listen to the words. Then listen and repeat.
Activities

1. read the newspaper	Do you read the newspaper?
2. play an instrument	Do you play an instrument?
3. dance	Do you dance?
4. play cards	Do you play cards?
5. take pictures	Do you take pictures?
6. listen to music	Do you listen to music?
7. play soccer	Do you play soccer?
8. tell stories	Do you tell stories?
9. ride a bicycle	Do you ride a bicycle?
10. have picnics	Do you have picnics?

Feelings

11. happy	Are you happy?
12. sad	Are you sad?
13. angry	Are you angry?
14. afraid	Are you afraid?
15. confused	Are you confused?

Lesson 7: 1. Listening Review (page 100)
Listen to the conversation. To finish the conversation, listen and choose the correct answer: A, B, or C. Use the Answer Sheet.

1. Hello. Is Lily there?

   A. No, I'm sorry. She's not home.
   B. What's your phone number?
   C. Call Jeff at 555-7723.

2. Who's calling, please?

   A. I think you have the wrong number.
   B. This is Maria. I'm her classmate.
   C. Just a minute. I'll get her.

3. A: He's not here right now. Can I take a message?

   A. Yes, please. Ask him to call Dr. Smith.
   B. Right. Thank you.
   C. You're welcome.

4. A: I love weekends.
   B: Really? What do you usually do?

   A. He's cooking dinner.
   B. I usually play soccer.
   C. No, I don't.

5. A: I live in Madison.
   B: Who do you live with?

   A. I pay the bills.
   B. I don't have a brother.
   C. My parents and my sister.

Lesson 7: 2. Dictation (page 100)
Listen and write the questions you hear. Then write your answers.

   1. What is your mother's name?
   2. What is your father's name?
   3. Do you have a sister?
   4. Do you clean the house?
   5. Do you wash the dishes?

UNIT EIGHT

Lesson 1: 4. Listen and Circle (page 102)
Listen to the conversations. Circle the body part that hurts.

1.
   A: Hi Melissa. Are you OK?
   B: No, my stomach hurts.

2.
   A: What's the matter, Tom? Does your ear hurt?
   B: No, my head hurts.
   A: Oh, I'm sorry.

3.
   A: Lisa, does your neck hurt?
   B: No, my throat hurts. I need to go home.

4.
   A: What's wrong?
   B: My knee hurts.
   A: Can you move it?
   B: No, I think it's broken.

Lesson 2: 1. Learn New Words (page 104)
Look at the picture. Listen to the words. Then listen and repeat.

   1. headache   Tina has a headache.
   2. earache   Martin's son has an earache.
   3. fever   Louis has a fever.
   4. runny nose   Ken has a runny nose.
   5. cough   Rose's daughter has a cough.
   6. sore throat   Donna has a sore throat.
   7. backache   Erik has a backache.
   8. sprained ankle David has a sprained ankle.
   9. stomachache   Tom has a stomachache.
   10. check-in desk Tina is standing at the check-in desk.
   11. waiting room   People are in the waiting room.
   12. examining room Louis is in the examining room.

Lesson 2: 4. Listen and Check (page 104)
Listen to the sentences. Look at the picture.
Check True or False.

   1. David has a sprained ankle.
   2. Tina is in an examining room.
   3. Rose's daughter has a stomachache.
   4. Erik has a backache.
   5. Ken is at the check-in desk.
   6. Donna is in the waiting room.

Lesson 4: 1. Learn New Words (page 108)
Look at the pictures. Listen to the words. Then listen and repeat.

   1. prescription medicine   It's a prescription medicine.
   2. tablets   Take two tablets.
   3. directions   Read the directions.
   4. drops   Take three drops.
   5. over-the-counter medicine It's an over-the-counter medicine.
   6. teaspoon   Take one teaspoon.

Lesson 5: 1. Practice Pronunciation: Linking Vowel to Vowel with a Y or W Sound (page 110)
B. Listen and complete the conversations. Then practice them with a partner.

1.
   A: This is 9-1-1.
   B: My mother is hurt. She is choking.
   A: Where are you?
   B: I am at 414 Pine Street.

2.
A: Where are you?
B: I am at home.
A: How is Paul?
B: He is resting.

Lesson 7: 1. Listening Review (page 114)
You will hear a question. Listen to the conversation. You will hear the question again. Choose the correct answer: A, B, or C. Use the Answer Sheet.

1.What's the problem?
   A: My wrist hurts.
   B: Can you move it?
   A: No, I can't.

What's the problem?
   A. He can't move his ankle.
   B. His arm hurts.
   C. His wrist hurts.

2.What's the matter?
   A: I'm sick.
   B: What's wrong?
   A: I have a stomachache.
   B: Do you have a headache, too?
   A: No, I don't.

What's the matter?
   A. He has a headache.
   B. He has a stomachache.
   C. He has an earache.

3.What should he do?
   A: What's wrong?
   B: I have a fever and a headache.
   A: You should take aspirin and rest.

What should he do?
   A. He should take aspirin and eat soft food.
   B. He should rest and use ear drops.
   C. He should rest and take aspirin.

4.What's wrong?
   A: We need an ambulance quickly! My brother is bleeding!
   B: Where are you?
   A: We're at 145 Jackson Street.

What's wrong?
   A. Her brother is bleeding.
   B. Her brother isn't breathing.
   C. Her brother is at 145 Jackson Street.

5.What should he do?
   A: My ankle hurts.
   B: You should bandage it.
   A: Okay.
   B: You should put ice on it, too.

What should he do?
   A. He should put heat on it and take aspirin.
   B. He should put ice on it and keep it dry.
   C. He should bandage it and put ice on it.

Lesson 7: 2. Dictation (page 114)
Listen and write the sentences you hear.

1. I have a fever.
2. She's having a heart attack.
3. You should put ice on your ankle.
4. Should I take cough medicine?
5. Drink liquids and rest.

UNIT NINE

Lesson 1: 1. Learn New Words (page 116)
Look at the pictures. Listen to the words. Then listen and repeat.

1. sofa	The sofa is in the living room.
2. bookcase	The bookcase is in the living room.
3. lamp	The lamp is in the living room.
4. television	The television is in the living room.
5. coffee table	The coffee table is in the living room.
6. plant	The plant is in the living room.
7. smoke alarm	The smoke alarm is in the dining room.
8. rug	The rug is in the dining room.
9. mirror	The mirror is in the bathroom.
10. sink	The sink is in the bathroom.
11. shower	The shower is in the bathroom.
12. toilet	The toilet is in the bathroom.
13. bathtub	The bathtub is in the bathroom.
14. drawer	The drawer is in the kitchen.
15. cabinet	The cabinet is in the kitchen.
16. closet	The closet is in the kitchen.
17. refrigerator	The refrigerator is in the kitchen.
18. stove	The stove is in the kitchen.
19. dresser	The dresser is in the bedroom.
20. bed	The bed is in the bedroom.

Lesson 2: 1. Learn New Words (page 118)
Look at the pictures. Listen to the words. Then listen and repeat.

Picture A: The Lees' Old House

1. porch	The Lees' old house had a porch.
2. garden	The Lees' old house had a garden.
3. backyard	The Lees' old house had a backyard.
4. garage	The Lees' old house had a garage.
5. fence	The Lees' old house had a fence.
6. gate	The Lees' old house had a gate in the fence.
7. mailbox	The Lees' old house had a mailbox.

Picture B: The Lees' New House

8. patio	The Lees' new house has a patio.
9. pool	The Lees' new house has a pool.
10. carport	The Lees' new house has a carport.
11. driveway	The Lees' new house has a driveway.
12. front yard	The Lees' new house has a front yard.

Lesson 2: 2. Listen and Check (page 118)
Listen to the sentences. Check Old House or New House.

1. There is a car in the carport.
2. There is a garden in the backyard.
3. There is a car in the driveway.
4. There is a pool in the backyard.
5. There is a side porch.
6. There is a fence in the front yard.

Lesson 3: 2. Listen and Match (page 120)
Look at the pictures. Listen to the conversations. Match each conversation with a person.

1.
A: What happened?
B: I cut my hand yesterday.
A: How?
B: I was cutting bread.

2.
A: What happened to you?
B: I fell off a chair this morning.
A: Are you okay?
B: Yes, I'm okay. Thanks.

3.
A: Hi! What happened?
B: I sprained my ankle.
A: How?
B: I fell off a ladder on Saturday.
A: Oh no!

4.
A: Is your leg broken?
B: Yes, it is.
A: What happened?
B: I fell down the stairs.

5.
A: Are you okay?
B: Yes, my ankle hurts, but I'm okay.
A: What happened?
B: I tripped on a rug in the living room.

6.
A: My back hurts.
B: Why? What happened?
A: I slipped in the shower this morning.
B: Oh no! You should go to the hospital.

Lesson 4: 1. Learn New Words (page 122)
Look at the pictures. Listen to the words. Then listen and repeat.

1. apartment   Do you live in an apartment?
2. condo   Do you live in a condo?
3. mobile home   Do you live in a mobile home?

Lesson 6: 1. Learn New Words (page 126)
Look at the bills. Listen to the words. Then listen and repeat.

1. gas and electric   John pays his gas and electric bill.
2. cable   John has cable television.
3. bill   John pays his bill every month.
4. account number   John's account number is 6464560483-0.
5. amount due   The amount due is $133.19.
6. amount enclosed   The amount enclosed is $133.19.
7. new charges   The amount of new charges is $56.29.

Lesson 7: 1. Listening Review (page 128)
Listen to the conversation. To finish the conversation, listen and choose the correct answer: A, B, or C. Use the Answer Sheet.

1.
A: How much is the rent for the two-bedroom apartment?
B: It's $900 a month. Would you like to see it?

A. Yes, it is.
B. Yes, I would.
C. Yes, it has two bedrooms.

2.
A: May I speak with Mr. Brown?
B: This is Mr. Brown.
A: I'm calling about the apartment for rent. Is it still available?

A. It has two bedrooms.
B. Yes, it is.
C. It's $1,150 a month.

3.
A: What happened to Noah?
B: He slipped in the shower.

A. Is he okay?
B. Are you okay?
C. Would you like to see it?

4.
A: Sue broke her leg.
B: What happened to her?

A. Is she okay now?
B. He tripped on the rug.
C. She fell down the stairs.

5.
A: I'm calling about the house for rent. Is it still available?
B: Yes, it is.
A: Can you tell me a little bit more about it?

A. No, it doesn't have a garage.
B. Yes, I would like to see it.
C. Sure, it has a big front yard, a garden, and a garage.

Lesson 7: 2. Dictation (page 128)
Listen and write the sentences you hear.

1. The new television is in the living room.
2. Her old house had a large patio, a garden, and a pool.
3. This condo has a garage and a big side patio.
4. He fell down the stairs this morning.
5. Would you like to see the apartment today?

UNIT TEN

Lesson 1: 1 Learn New Words (page 130)
Look at the pictures. Listen to the words. Then listen and repeat.

Indoor jobs

1. chef	Adam is a chef. He cooked food today.
2. office manager	Anita is an office manager. She used a computer, a fax machine, and a photocopier today.
3. plumber	Sam is a plumber. He repaired sinks and toilets today.
4. home healthcare provider	Julie is a home healthcare provider. She took care of sick people in their homes today.

Indoor/Outdoor jobs

5. childcare worker	Tony is a childcare worker. He took care of children today.
6. mechanic	Mike is a mechanic. He fixed cars today.
7. mover	Jack is a mover. He lifted heavy things today.

Outdoor jobs

8. construction worker	Dan is a construction worker. He built buildings today.
9. truck driver	Bill is a truck driver. He drove a truck today.
10. landscaper	Alan is a landscaper. He took care of plants today.

Lesson 1: 4 Listen and Match (page 130–131)
Listen to the conversations. Match the jobs to the conversations.

1.
A: How was your day today?
B: It was great! I fixed three cars and one truck today.

2.
A: How many people did you take care of today?
B: Two. I was at Mrs. Wong's house in the morning and Mr. Brady's house in the afternoon.

3.
A: What's wrong?
B: I hurt my back. I lifted a heavy couch this afternoon.

4.
A: You look tired. What's wrong?
B: I repaired three toilets and seven sinks today! It was a long day!

5.
A: I saw your sister today.
B: Really? Where did you see her?
A: I saw her with a group of children at the daycare center.

Lesson 3: 1. Learn New Words
(page 134)
Look at the picture. Listen to the words. Then listen and repeat.

1. job fair	People are at the job fair.
2. chew gum	Someone is chewing gum.
3. dress neatly	The man in the suit is dressed neatly.
4. shake hands	The men are shaking hands.
5. interview	The man is having a job interview.
6. résumé	Tim is holding a résumé.

Lesson 3: 4 Listen and Take Notes (page 134)
Listen to Rosa's job interview. Write the missing information.

Interviewer: So, Rosa, tell me about yourself.
Rosa: Well, I'm really interested in retail. Right now I'm the store manager at Lane's. I got the job in 2008.
Interviewer: That's very interesting. Do you like your job?
Rosa: Yes, very much. I'm really sad Lane's is closing soon.
Interviewer: Yes, that is too bad. And what did you do before that?
Rosa: Well, I was a salesclerk at Lane's for almost four years, from 2004 to 2008. Then I got promoted to store manager.
Interviewer: Yes, I see.
Rosa: And before that, I worked as a salesclerk at a store called The Elephant's Trunk.
Interviewer: When was that?
Rosa: I worked there from 2002 to 2004. I learned a lot there.

Lesson 7: 1. Listening Review (page 143)
Look at the pictures and listen. Choose the correct answer: A, B, or C. Use the Answer Sheet.

1.
A: What do you do?
B: I'm a landscaper.

2.
A: What's your job?
B: I'm a childcare worker.

3.
A: What did you do at your last job?
B: I was a plumber.

4.

   A: What was your last job?
   B: I was a construction worker.

5.

   A: Why should I hire you?
   B: Because I'm a hard worker and I listen carefully.
   A: Great. You're hired.

Lesson 7: 2. Dictation (page 142)
Listen and write the questions you hear.

   1. Did you drive a car yesterday?
   2. What was your last job?
   3. What are you going to do next week?

VOCABULARY LIST

Numbers in parentheses indicate unit numbers.

A.M. (3)
account number (3)
account number (9)
across from (2)
address (1)
afraid (7)
after (3)
afternoon (3)
aisle (6)
am (1)
ambulance (2)
ambulance (8)
amount (3)
amount due (9)
amount enclosed (9)
angry (7)
ankle (8)
anything (6)
apartment (9)
appetizers (6)
apple (6)
appointment (4)
April (4)
are (1)
area code (1)
arm (8)
ask (1)
aspirin (8)
assistant (10)
ATM (2)
audio CDs (2)
August (4)
aunt (7)
authorization (10)
available (9)
avoid (8)
back (8)
backache (8)
backyard (9)
bag (6)
baked potato (6)
bakery (6)
banana (6)
bandage (8)
bank (2)
baseball cap (5)
basket (6)
basketball game (4)
bathtub (9)
bean (6)
bed (9)
benefits (10)
between (2)
beverages (6)
bill (3)
bill (9)
birthday party (4)
birthplace (1)

black (5)
bleed (8)
blue (5)
board (1)
book (1)
bookbag (1)
bookcase (9)
boots (5)
borrow (10)
bottle (6)
box (6)
bread (6)
briefs (5)
brother (7)
brown (5)
build (10)
bus (2)
bus driver (1)
bus stop (2)
butter (6)
buying (5)
cabinet (9)
cable (9)
can (6)
cancel (4)
capital (2)
car (2)
carbon monoxide detector (7)
carpet (9)
carport (9)
carrot (6)
cart (6)
carton (6)
cashier (1)
cashier (5)
cell phone (3)
cents (3)
cereal (6)
chair (1)
cheap (6)
check (3)
check number (3)
check out (6)
check-in desk (8)
checkout counter (6)
checkout desk (2)
cheese (6)
chef (10)
chest (8)
chew gum (10)
chicken (6)
child safety seat (7)
childcare worker (10)
children (7)
choke (8)
circle (1)
city (1)
clean the house (7)

clock (1)
close (1)
closed (3)
closet (9)
cloudy (4)
coat (5)
coffee (6)
coffee table (9)
coin (3)
cold (4)
coming into (5)
comma (1)
community center (2)
computer (1)
computer class (4)
condo (9)
confused (7)
construction worker (10)
contact (8)
cook (10)
cook dinner (7)
cool (4)
corn (6)
cough (8)
country (1)
coupons (6)
cousin (7)
crosswalk (2)
cup (6)
customer (5)
customer service (5)
cut (9)
cutting (5)
dairy (6)
dance (7)
date of birth (1)
daughter (7)
deadbolt lock (7)
December (4)
deductions (3)
dental appointment (4)
dentist (1)
department store (5)
desk (1)
dime (3)
directions (8)
divorced (1)
do not enter (2)
do the laundry (7)
doctor (1)
doctor's appointment (4)
document (10)
dollar (3)
door (1)
drawer (9)
dress (5)
dress neatly (10)
dresser (9)

drink (8)
drive (10)
driver's license (10)
driveway (9)
drops (8)
drugstore (2)
dry (8)
ear (8)
earache (8)
east (2)
eat (6)
eating (3)
eight (1)
eighteen (3)
eighteenth (4)
eighth (4)
eighty (3)
elbow (8)
eleven (1)
eleven (3)
eleventh (4)
emergency (8)
employment (10)
enter (2)
entrance (5)
eraser (1)
evening (3)
examining room (8)
exit (5)
expensive (6)
extra large (5)
eye (8)
fall (9)
farmers' market (6)
fast-food restaurant (10)
father (7)
fax machine (10)
February (4)
federal tax (3)
feed the pets (7)
feet (8)
fell (9)
female (1)
fence (7)
fence (9)
fever (8)
fifteen (3)
fifteenth (4)
fifth (4)
fifty (3)
fine (1)
finger (8)
fire extinguisher (7)
fire station (2)
fireplace (9)
first (4)
fish (6)
fitting room (5)

fitting room attendant (5)
five (1)
fix things (7)
flammable (8)
floor (1)
food (6)
foot (8)
foreign (10)
forty (3)
four (1)
fourteen (1)
fourteen (3)
fourteenth (4)
fourth (4)
Friday (3)
front yard (9)
fruit (6)
future (10)
gallon (8)
garage (9)
garden (9)
gas and electric (9)
gas station (2)
gate (9)
gender (1)
go grocery shopping (7)
go to (1)
going into (5)
grain (6)
granddaughter (7)
grandfather (7)
grandmother (7)
grandson (7)
grape (6)
green (5)
gross pay (3)
haircut appointment (4)
hamburger (6)
hand (8)
handrail (7)
happy (7)
hat (5)
have picnics (7)
head (6)
head (8)
headache (8)
heart attack (8)
heat (8)
heavy (10)
helping (5)
hire (10)
hole (5)
home healthcare provider (10)
honey (6)
hospital (2)
hot (4)
hours (3)
house (9)
husband (7)
ice (6)

ice cream (6)
identification (10)
improve (10)
in back of (2)
in front of (2)
indoor (10)
inhale (8)
internally (8)
interview (10)
is (1)
jacket (5)
January (4)
jar (6)
jeans (5)
job fair (10)
job interview (4)
juice (6)
July (4)
June (4)
knee (8)
knife (9)
label (8)
ladder (9)
lamp (9)
landscaper (10)
large (5)
laundromat (2)
leaving (5)
left (2)
leg (8)
lettuce (6)
librarian (2)
library (2)
library card (2)
lift (10)
like (6)
liquids (8)
listen (1)
listen carefully (10)
listen to music (7)
loaf (6)
long (5)
look at (6)
loose (5)
macaroni and cheese (6)
machinist (1)
magazine (2)
mailbox (2)
mailbox (9)
main courses (6)
make the bed (7)
male (1)
manager (6)
map (1)
March (4)
marital status (1)
married (1)
May (4)
meat (6)
mechanic (10)

medicine (8)
medium (5)
memo (3)
menu (6)
middle name (1)
midnight (3)
milk (6)
minute (3)
mirror (9)
mobile home (9)
Monday (3)
month (4)
morning (3)
mother (7)
mouth (8)
mover (10)
movie theater (2)
Mr. (1)
Mrs. (1)
Ms. (1)
near (2)
neck (8)
necktie (5)
nephew (7)
net pay (3)
never (7)
new charges (9)
next to (2)
nickel (3)
niece (7)
night (3)
nine (1)
nineteen (3)
nineteenth (4)
ninety (3)
ninth (4)
no left turn (2)
no parking (2)
no right turn (2)
noodles (6)
noon (3)
north (2)
nose (8)
notebook (1)
November (4)
nurse (1)
nut (6)
o'clock (3)
occupation (1)
October (4)
office manager (10)
often (7)
oil (6)
on sale (6)
on the corner of (2)
one (1)
one hundred (3)
one way (2)
onion (6)
onion rings (6)

open (1)
open (3)
orange (6)
ounce (6)
outdoor (10)
over-the-counter (8)
P.M. (3)
package (6)
pants (5)
parents (7)
park (2)
parking lot (2)
partner (1)
passport (10)
patio (9)
pay phone (2)
pay rate (3)
pay the bills (7)
peanut (6)
pen (1)
pencil (1)
penny (3)
period (1)
permanent (10)
pharmacist (1)
piece of paper (1)
pint (8)
pizza (6)
plant (9)
play an instrument (7)
play cards (7)
play soccer (7)
playground (2)
plumber (10)
poison (8)
police officer (1)
police station (2)
pool (9)
porch (9)
post office (2)
pound (6)
practice (1)
pregnant (8)
prescription (8)
price tag (5)
produce section (6)
promoted (10)
PTA meeting (4)
purple (5)
push a cart (6)
quart (8)
quarter (3)
question mark (1)
rainy (4)
raise (1)
read (1)
read the newspaper (7)
receipt (5)
red (5)
refrigerator (9)

rent (9)
repair (10)
repeat (1)
reschedule (4)
resident (10)
rest (8)
restaurant (10)
restaurant (2)
resume (10)
rice (6)
ride a bicycle (7)
right (2)
rug (9)
running (5)
runny nose (8)
sad (7)
safety gate (7)
safety lock (7)
salad (6)
salesclerk (1)
salon (10)
sandwich (6)
Saturday (3)
say (1)
school (2)
scissors (5)
second (4)
September (4)
seven (1)
seventeen (3)
seventeenth (4)
seventh (4)
seventy (3)
shake hands (10)
shirt (5)
shoes (5)
short (5)
shorts (5)
shoulder (8)
shower (9)
side dishes (6)
sidewalk (2)

signature (3)
single (1)
sink (9)
sister (7)
sit down (1)
six (1)
sixteen (3)
sixteenth (4)
sixth (4)
sixty (3)
size (5)
skirt (5)
sleeping (5)
slice (6)
slip (9)
small (5)
smoke alarm (9)
smoke detector (7)
smoking (3)
sneakers (5)
snowy (4)
socks (5)
soda (6)
sofa (9)
soft food (8)
sometimes (7)
son (7)
sore (8)
soup (6)
south (2)
sprained ankle (8)
stairs (9)
stand in line (6)
stand up (1)
state (1)
state tax (3)
stomach (8)
stomachache (8)
stop (2)
stoplight (2)
stove (9)
street (1)

student (1)
stylist (10)
sugar (6)
Sunday (3)
sunny (4)
supermarket (2)
sweater (5)
table (1)
tablet (8)
tailor (5)
take care of (10)
take out (1)
take out the trash (7)
take pictures (7)
talking (5)
taxi (2)
tea (6)
teacher (1)
teaspoon (8)
teeth (8)
telephone number (1)
television (9)
tell stories (7)
ten (1)
tenth (4)
third (4)
thirteen (1)
thirteen (3)
thirteenth (4)
thirtieth (4)
thirty (3)
three (1)
throat (8)
Thursday (3)
tight (5)
toe (8)
toilet (9)
tomato (6)
too (5)
tooth (8)
transportation (7)
trip (9)

truck (2)
truck driver (10)
trying on (5)
T-shirt (5)
Tuesday (3)
turn (2)
twelfth (4)
twelve (1)
twelve (3)
twentieth (4)
twenty (3)
twenty-one (3)
twenty-two (3)
two (1)
uncle (7)
unconscious (8)
undershirt (5)
vegetable (6)
vending machine (2)
video DVDs (2)
waiting room (8)
wall (1)
warm (4)
wash the dishes (7)
wearing (5)
weather (4)
Wednesday (3)
west (2)
white (5)
wife (7)
window (1)
window guard (7)
windy (4)
wrist (8)
write (1)
yellow (5)
yogurt (6)
zero (1)
zip code (1)

IRREGULAR VERBS

Irregular Verbs

Base Form	Simple Past	Base Form	Simple Past
be	was/were	keep	kept
become	became	know	knew
begin	began	leave	left
bleed	bled	lend	lent
break	broke	lose	lost
bring	brought	make	made
buy	bought	meet	met
choose	chose	pay	paid
come	came	put	put
cost	cost	read	read
cut	cut	ring	rang
do	did	run	ran
drink	drank	see	saw
drive	drove	sell	sold
eat	ate	send	sent
fall	fell	set	set
feel	felt	shake	shook
fight	fought	shut	shut
find	found	sleep	slept
forget	forgot	speak	spoke
fry	fried	speed	sped
get	got	spend	spent
give	gave	take	took
go	went	teach	taught
grow	grew	tell	told
have/has	had	think	thought
hear	heard	wear	wore
hold	held	write	wrote
hurt	hurt		

CREDITS

SKILLS INDEX

ACADEMIC SKILLS

Grammar
A/an, 66, 169
Adjectives,
    demonstrative, 64, 168
    + noun, 52, 164
    order of, 116, 186
    possessive, 11, 149
Adverbs,
    of frequency, 92, 178
    of manner, 134, 194
And, 94, 180
Articles
    a/an, 66, 169
Be, 4, 144
    + *going to,* 136, 195, 196
    simple past of, 118, 187–188
    wh- questions, 18, 46, 150–151
    yes/no questions with, 156–157
But, 94, 180
Can or *can't,* 102, 181–182
    questions with, 104, 183
    requests and offers with, 122, 191
Capitalization, 24, 155, 160
Compound sentences, 94, 180
Continuous, present, 61, 62, 165–166, 167
Contractions, 145, 152, 165
Count and noncount nouns, 76, 172
Demonstratives, 64, 168
Frequency, adverbs of, 92, 178
Future with:
    be going to, 136, 195, 196
    will, 132, 193
Going to, future with, 136, 195, 196
Have, simple present of, 88, 175
How much/how many, 36, 158
Irregular:
    adverbs, 194
    verbs, simple past of, 131, 192
It's, 32
-ly, 194
Manner, adverbs of, 134, 194
May, 191
Negative statements, 146, 165, 171, 173,
    188, 193
Nouns,
    adjectives +, 52, 164
    capitalization of, 160
    count and noncount, 76, 172
    possessive, 14, 48, 161
    proper, 38, 160
    singular and plural, 9, 148, 161

Object pronouns, 108, 185
Offers with *can, may,* and *would like*
    122, 191
Past, simple, 118, 120, 131, 187–188,
    189–190 192
Place,
    capitalization of names of, 160
    prepositions of, 6, 20, 147, 152
Plural nouns, 9, 148, 161
Possessive:
    adjectives, 11, 149
    nouns, 14, 48, 161
Possessive with 's 14
Prepositions, 6, 20, 147, 152, 162
Present tense,
    continuous, 61, 62, 165–166, 167
    simple. *See* Simple present
Pronouns, object/subject, 108, 145, 185
Proper and common nouns, 38, 160
Punctuation, 155, 161
Questions,
    with *can* or *can't,* 104, 183
    with *how much/how many,* 36, 158
    in the present, 62, 150, 156, 167
    punctuation with, 155
    with *there is/are,* 154
    with *wh-* words, 18, 46, 80, 150, 174
    yes/no, 34, 90, 156, 176, 196
Regular verbs, simple past of, 120, 189
Requests with *can, may,* and *would like,*
    122, 191
's, use of, 14
Should or *shouldn't,* 106, 184
Simple past, 118, 120, 131, 187–188,
    189–190 192
Simple present, 4, 74, 170–171
    of *be,* 4, 18, 144
    of *have,* 88, 175
    wh- questions with, 18, 80, 150, 174
    yes/no questions with, 176
There is/there are, 22, 153, 154
This, that, these, those, 64, 168
Time, 162
Titles (*Mr., Dr.,* etc.), 160
Want, 78, 173
Wh- questions, 18, 80, 150, 174
Will, 132, 193
Would like, 122, 191
Yes/No questions, 34, 90, 156, 176, 196

Reading
Ads, 15, 122–123, 132–133
Calendars, 56

Checks, 38–39
Dates, 52–53
Descriptions, 94–95, 140
Forms, 10
Graphs, 120–121
Labels, 108–109, 112–113
Maps, 4–5, 21, 24–25
Memos, 71
Paystubs, 43
Questions and answers, 28–29
Store flyers, 80–81
Stories, 66–67, 136–137
Telephone books, 18
Utility bills, 126–127
Websites, 99

Writing
Abbreviations, 10
Advertisements, 122
Brainstorming, 122
Capitalization, 24
Charts, completing, 8, 15, 38, 57, 60, 78, 80,
    94, 106, 108, 130, 132, 134
Checks,
    bank, 38–39, 127
    guest, 84
Dates, 51, 52
Descriptions, 4, 60, 66, 70, 71, 116
Dictations, 16, 30, 32, 41, 44, 58, 72, 100,
    114, 128, 142
Forms, filling out, 10–11, 29, 140–141
Instructions, 8, 108
Job application, 140–141
Names, 3
Numbers, 36, 43
Punctuation, 10, 38, 66
Store receipt, 64
Time, 34, 41
Writing tips, 10, 24, 38, 52, 66, 80, 108,
    122, 136

Speaking
Alphabet, 2
Asking questions, 4, 6, 14, 46, 102
Asking where things are, 6
Giving opinions, 134
Instructions, 8–9
Learning about someone, 4, 90, 92, 106, 130
Talking about what you see, 20, 24, 34,
    62, 66, 76, 104, 116, 118, 134, 136
Practice Conversations
Answering requests for information, 27, 64,
    85, 132, 139